Vegetarian Pyramid Foods

There are many foods to choose from in a vegetarian diet, as you can see from the list below. Choose from the lower half of the pyramid most often (see the Vegetarian Food Guide Pyramid, pictured *opposite*):

♣ **Whole Grains:** Includes cereals such as wheat, corn, oats, rice, millet, and cereal products such as bread, tortillas, and pasta. Choose whole wheat or whole grain products most often.

♣ **Legumes (lehg-YOOMS):** Includes beans and peas such as soy, kidney, navy, pintos, split peas, lentils, black-eyed peas, and garbanzos. Also includes soy products such as tofu, soy beverages, and texturized protein foods. The peanut is also a legume but is often inaccurately identified as a nut.

♣ **Vegetables:** Choose from all vegetables including starchy vegetables such as potatoes and yams

♣ **Fruits:** Choose whole fruit rather than juice when possible (whole fruits contain fiber).

♣ **Nuts and Seeds:** Also includes nut butters and spreads. Although nuts are high in fat, it's a heart-healthier type of fat called monounsaturated fat. Choose raw or dry roasted nuts rather than oil roasted nuts most often.

♣ **Vegetable Oils:** Choose those that are high in monounsaturates such as olive, canola, or sesame. Limit use of tropical oils such as coconut, palm, and palm kernel oils.

♣ **Dairy:** Choose non- or low-fat products most often. If dairy is not consumed, women, teenagers, children, and the elderly should consider an alternate source or supplement of calcium and vitamin D.

♣ **Eggs:** Limit use of whole eggs or use egg whites only.

♣ **Sweets:** Eat in moderation.

Better Homes and Gardens®

Low-Fat & Luscious Vegetarian

Better Homes and Gardens® Books
Des Moines, Iowa

Better Homes and Gardens® Books
An imprint of Meredith® Books

Low-Fat & Luscious Vegetarian
Editor: Kristi M. Fuller, R.D.
Contributing Editors: Marsha Hudnall, R.D.; Shelli McConnell;
   Spectrum Communication Services, Inc.
Associate Art Director: Lynda Haupert
Copy Chief: Angela K. Renkoski
Contributing Copy Editor: Rosanne Mattson
Contributing Proofreader: Marcia R. Gilmer
Electronic Production Coordinator: Paula Forest
Editorial and Design Assistants: Judy Bailey, Jennifer Norris, Karen Schirm
Test Kitchen Director: Sharon Stilwell
Test Kitchen Product Supervisor: Marilyn Cornelius
Food Stylists: Susan Brosious, Sue Finley
Production Director: Douglas M. Johnston
Production Manager: Pam Kvitne
Assistant Prepress Manager: Marjorie J. Schenkelberg

Meredith® Books
Editor in Chief: James D. Blume
Design Director: Matt Strelecki
Managing Editor: Gregory H. Kayko
Executive Food Editor: Lisa Holderness

Director, Sales & Marketing, Retail: Michael A. Peterson
Director, Sales & Marketing, Special Markets: Rita McMullen
Director, Sales & Marketing, Home & Garden Center Channel: Ray Wolf
Director, Operations: Valerie Wiese

Vice President, General Manager: Jamie L. Martin

Better Homes and Gardens® Magazine
Editor in Chief: Jean LemMon
Executive Food Editor: Nancy Byal

Meredith® Publishing Group
President, Publishing Group: Christopher M. Little
Vice President and Publishing Director: John P. Loughlin

Meredith® Corporation
Chairman of the Board: Jack D. Rehm
President and Chief Executive Officer: William T. Kerr

Chairman of the Executive Committee: E. T. Meredith III

All of us at Better Homes and Gardens® Books are dedicated to providing you with the information and ideas you need to create delicious foods. We welcome your comments and suggestions. Write to us at: Better Homes and Gardens® Books, Cookbook Editorial Department, RW–240, 1716 Locust St., Des Moines, IA 50309–3023.

If you would like to order additional copies of any of our books, check with your local bookstore.

Our seal assures you that every recipe in *Low-Fat & Luscious Vegetarian* has been tested in the Better Homes and Gardens® Test Kitchen. This means that each recipe is practical and reliable, and meets our high standards of taste appeal. We guarantee your satisfaction with this book for as long as you own it.

Photography: Tony Kubat Photography

Pictured on front cover: Indian-Style Vegetables and Rice
   (see recipe, page 118)
Pictured on page 3: Blue Cheese and Bean Salad
   (see recipe, page 48)

Contents

Try something exciting and new, like Breakfast Pizza (see recipe, page 16). Fresh ideas using eggs, "sausage," cereal, and more await you for breakfasts you'll remember.

You won't suffer any guilt here—just enjoy some of the best (healthful) nibbles around. (See Layered Southwestern Dip, page 30).

You can't go wrong with a huge salad full of crisp greens and vegetables. (Tip: Go easy on the dressings.) Fresh, cool salads make great meals any time of year. (See Tortellini Vegetable Salad, page 58.)

Sometimes a bowl of steaming soup is all you need for a satisfying meal. Choose from many favorite and new soups. (See Succotash Soup and Dumplings, page 75.)

Vegetarian Varieties

♣ **Vegan:** Eats only plant-based foods

♣ **Lacto-Vegetarian:** Includes milk and milk products in the diet

♣ **Ovo-Vegetarian:** Includes eggs

♣ **Lacto-Ovo Vegetarian:** Includes milk, milk products, and eggs in meals

♣ **Pollo-Vegetarian:** Includes poultry in addition to the above

♣ **Pesca-Vegetarian:** Includes fish and other seafood in the diet but no poultry or meat products

♣ **Occasional Vegetarian:** Chooses a "plant-centered" diet along with small amounts of animal-derived products or less use of those products

The Joy of Eating ...Vegetarian!

Only a few short years ago a meal without meat wouldn't pass muster in many American homes. But today, increasingly nutrition-conscious people of all ages are going vegetarian. Why? Because it's good for you, but also because we now have access to such a variety of fruits, vegetables, beans, and grains, that vegetarian eating has become more pleasurable. Forget the textured vegetable protein of the '70s. Today your choice in vegetarian fare is limitless—and definitely luscious.

The health benefits of a vegetarian diet are impressive. Imagine reducing your chances of developing heart disease, colon cancer, high blood pressure, diabetes, and obesity—just by passing on the meat in favor of enticing choices such as Roasted Hot Potato Salad, Curried Lentil Stew, Vegetable Nachos, Portobello Mushroom Stroganoff, or Southwestern Enchilada Skillet.

Are these benefits real or is vegetarianism just another diet fad full of empty promises? Most nutrition experts agree vegetarianism definitely offers significant health-promoting benefits. However, as with most diet and health issues, it's necessary to keep in mind a few fine points.

Although vegetarians, particularly those who eat no animal products at all, generally suffer fewer of the chronic diseases that plague Americans, it's not entirely clear whether they are healthier only because of what they eat. Their good health could be due to other things they do or be the result of a combination of diet and

behavior. For instance, it has been found that vegetarians generally have healthier lifestyles—they smoke less, exercise more, and tend to weigh in at healthier numbers than nonvegetarians. These behaviors exert powerful, positive effects on health.

It's important, too, to understand that you'll only gain the potential disease-fighting benefits of a vegetarian diet if—and it's a big if—your diet is nutritionally balanced. Going vegetarian is not just a matter of giving up meat. In fact, in their initial efforts to go vegetarian, many people stumble over the same nutritional obstacle that stymies many meat eaters: excessive dietary fat. Too much oil, nuts, full-fat cheese, butter, cream and other high-fat ingredients may cancel the advantages of vegetarian eating.

Indeed, many popular vegetarian cookbooks available today help guide novice and experienced vegetarians in exploring plant-based cuisine but may contain recipes that are heavy in fat. *Low-Fat and Luscious Vegetarian,* however, features recipes developed with health in mind. Fresh, familiar, and easily obtained ingredients are the basis for this collection of tasty recipes designed to help devout and occasional vegetarians reap the benefits of a vegetarian diet.

On the following pages, we tell you how to plan a healthful vegetarian diet. We also include a variety of tips for getting started—whether you're ready to go cold turkey (or should we say no turkey?) and never again eat meat, or you're just looking for ways to boost your family's health and increase their interest in mealtime by adding some meatless dishes to your menu repertoire. Whatever you choose, bon appetit—and here's to happy and healthy eating!

Vegetarianism at Its Best

There are several ways to go vegetarian (see Vegetarian Varieties, page 6), but they all share one characteristic. Vegetarian cooking is based on plant foods, which means plenty of grains (including whole grains), legumes (beans, and peas, soy products, and texturized protein foods), vegetables, and fruits. That's where many of the potential health benefits come from. In sufficient amounts, these foods combine to make up a diet low in fat but rich in fiber, vitamins, and minerals—just what health experts say is needed to reduce the chances of chronic diseases.

Plant foods may also offer an extra advantage in the fight against two of the major diseases affecting Americans. Plant foods contain beneficial compounds called phytochemicals ("plant chemicals") that appear to help fend off heart disease and cancer. You may have heard of at least two phytochemicals already: beta-carotene found in deep green and yellow-orange fruits and vegetables, and isoflavone genistein found in soybeans.

Prudent planning is the key to gaining the benefits of a plant-rich diet. Aim for balanced meals that feature a variety of foods. Strive to include the nutrients you need every day without going overboard on fat, saturated fat, or sodium, which may create or worsen health problems.

How do you design healthful meatless meals? Start by following the vegetarian version of The Food Guide Pyramid, developed by the U.S. Department of Agriculture (see The Vegetarian Pyramid, page 8 and on the inside of the front cover). Its principles are simple, whether you're a strict or a occasional vegetarian.

It doesn't matter what type of vegetarian you are. You take a big step toward boosting your health with any diet that includes plenty of grains (including whole grains), legumes, vegetables, and fruits.

Also, remember that too much oil, nuts, full-fat cheese, butter, cream and other high-fat ingredients may cancel the advantages of vegetarian eating.

Reduced risk of heart disease, cancer, high blood pressure, diabetes, and obesity: These noteworthy health benefits make it wise to choose vegetarian meals.

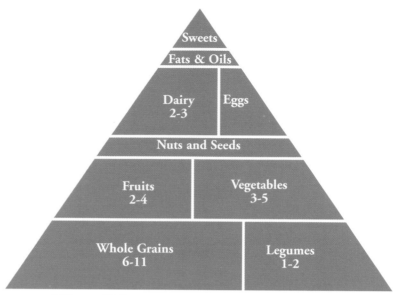

The Vegetarian Pyramid*

Principle #1: Eat a variety of foods daily from the lower four groups of the Pyramid and the Dairy and Eggs groups. The exception is for vegetarians who don't consume dairy products (see Principle #3). Their choices should primarily come from the other five groups mentioned. Use whole eggs, nuts, seeds, fats, oils, and sweets in moderation.

Principle #2: Move from the bottom up. Your meals should include more whole grain foods, legumes, vegetables, and fruits than other foods. Grains provide energy-rich carbohydrates, fiber, B vitamins, and iron. Grains and cereals such as wheat, corn, oats, and rice also contribute protein to the diet. Fruits and vegetables provide fiber and important vitamins and minerals. Frequently eat foods that contain vitamin C (such as citrus fruits, melons, green peppers, and broccoli) at the same time as you eat iron-rich foods (such as beans) to help your body absorb the iron more efficiently.

Principle #3: Choose at least two servings of low-fat or skim dairy products daily. Growing children, teenage girls, and women should aim for three servings daily to help ensure strong bones and teeth. Other high-calcium foods include calcium-fortified soy milk, cheese, and orange juice; tofu processed with calcium sulfate; and green, leafy vegetables. These foods are essential to ensure adequate calcium for vegetarians who do not consume milk and milk products.

Principle #4: Choose 2 to 3 servings from meat substitutes, such as beans, nuts, seeds, peanut butter, tofu, or eggs throughout the day. Contrary to past advice, it's not necessary to carefully mix and match protein sources as long as you eat a variety each day.

Principle #5: Choose sparingly from the tip of the Pyramid. Foods such as oil, butter, sodas, and candy supply calories but little nutrition.

*__Note:__ See inside front cover for examples from each food group.

For Special Consideration ...

The Vegetarian Pyramid outlines the basics of balanced vegetarian eating for healthy adults. In some instances, however, additional nutritional concerns may exist.

For example, vegans eat only plant foods. But plant foods don't supply vitamin B_{12}, which is essential to good health. Therefore, vegans need a reliable source of this vitamin, such as vitamin supplements or fortified foods such as fortified breakfast cereals, soy beverages, and brewer's yeast, in their diets. Read the labels of these products to determine how much you need to eat to reach 100 percent of the required amount of vitamin B_{12} each day. Spirulina, seaweed, tempeh, and other fermented foods are not reliable sources.

If you are a pregnant or breast-feeding vegan, you may also need a vitamin D supplement if you're not regularly exposed to sunlight or if you use sunblock (sunlight converts a provitamin in the skin into vitamin D). In addition, like nonvegetarians, pregnant and breast-feeding vegetarians of all types often are advised to take iron and folic acid supplements. You should also pay extra attention to getting adequate amounts of calcium and vitamin B_{12} in your diet. As always, however, if you are pregnant or breast-feeding, check with your doctor before taking supplements of any kind.

Children also have special needs that must be considered when they're eating vegetarian diets (see Children & Vegetarianism at right). In particular, make certain they get enough calories. Vegetarian diets are often bulky or filling, and children may have difficulty eating enough at one time to meet their energy needs. Frequent snacks and meals are recommended.

Don't give children foods that contain extra amounts of fiber unless your doctor or registered dietitian advises it. Substances found in these foods can limit iron and zinc absorption. A good rule of thumb for fiber intake is your child's age plus five. If your child is 5 years old, that means he or she shouldn't have more than 10 grams of fiber a day.

Pregnant and breast-feeding women, whether vegetarian or not, should follow a doctor's or registered dietitian's advice about good nutrition.

Children & Vegetarianism

Children are not small adults. Still, a vegetarian diet that meets the needs of healthy adults may also serve the needs of children older than 2 years. But as with adults, vegan diets for children require special attention. Follow these guidelines:

♣ **Children on vegan diets need to consume a reliable source of vitamin B_{12} each day.**

♣ **Vegan children may need a vitamin D supplement.**

♣ **To ensure adequate intakes of calcium, iron, and zinc, children on vegan diets must eat a variety of foods.**

♣ **Children need several snacks daily to make sure they get enough calories for growth.**

♣ **Young children pose special nutritional challenges. Seek the advice of a pediatrician or a registered dietitian when feeding infants or toddlers vegetarian diets.**

Vegetarian meals come together quickly when you rely on the many convenience products available at your supermarket.

♣ Check the deli for timesavers such as pasta salad or unbaked vegetable-topped pizzas.

♣ Stroll the frozen food section for cheese-filled pastas and breads, along with meat substitutes that look and taste as good as the real thing.

♣ Pick up easy-to-fix packaged grain and rice mixes, now available in a variety of flavors.

Going Vegetarian

Getting the benefits of vegetarian eating doesn't require totally giving up meat. Whether your goal is to move you and your family to a meat-free diet or to stop somewhere in between, try these tips to get started.

♣ Set aside one day a week at first to eat vegetarian. Meatless Mondays, perhaps? If a whole day is too much, start with one meal.

♣ Think of vegetarian meals your family already enjoys, such as pasta primavera, spaghetti with tomato sauce, and vegetable soup. Keep these on the menu as you explore new ideas.

♣ Serve new dishes alongside old family favorites. Try a vegetarian stew with garlic bread, salad, and ice cream.

♣ Serve breakfast for dinner. This is a great way to enjoy special treats such as French toast and waffles that busy mornings rule out.

♣ Instead of beef or chicken, try tofu. Tofu takes on the flavor of the foods it is cooked with. Try it in dishes such as stir-fries, dishes with a sauce, or soups.

♣ Go ethnic. Try Mexican bean burritos, Chinese fried rice, Middle East tabbouleh or hummus, and minestrone for an around-the-world vegetarian adventure.

♣ Get to know beans. There are dozens of varieties that offer different tastes and textures. Try a different bean each time you make your favorite chili or soup. Or, mix varieties for another twist.

♣ Trade pepperoni for a colorful mélange of your favorite vegetables on your next pizza. Top it with red onions; green, red, or yellow peppers; mushrooms; black olives; dried or fresh tomatoes; or artichoke hearts. If your local pizzeria is limited in choices, order a half-baked plain cheese pizza or pick up a fresh, unbaked one from the supermarket. Then devise your own vegetarian taste treat by topping it with a few sautéed vegetables such as sweet peppers, artichoke hearts, broccoli, leeks, or zucchini.

♣ Expand your taste horizons. Try a little almond, cashew, or other nut butters instead of peanut butter on rice cakes or fat-free whole wheat crackers.

What You'll Find in This Book

Thanks to the nutrition analyses provided in this book, it's easy to see the amount of fat (in grams) and the Percent Daily Value Fat and Saturated Fat* in each recipe. The nutrition analysis below shows an example of the Nutrition Facts listed with every recipe. Exchanges (based on the American Diabetes Association exchange system), useful for calorie-counters, are also listed with every recipe:

TOTAL FAT: **11 g**
DAILY VALUE FAT: **17%**
SATURATED FAT: **2 g**
DAILY VALUE SATURATED FAT: **10%**

NUTRITION FACTS PER SERVING

Calories	370
Total Fat	11 g
Saturated Fat	2 g
Cholesterol	45 mg
Sodium	563 mg
Carbohydrate	48 g
Fiber	2 g
Protein	22 g

EXCHANGES:
3 Starch
1 Medium-Fat Meat
1 Vegetable

Note: In this book and on today's food labels, the Percent Daily Value Fat is based on a daily intake of 2,000 calories, 65 grams fat,** and 20 grams saturated fat. In a hypothetical example of the nutrition analysis of a recipe, above, you can see that the recipe includes 11 grams of fat (17% of the 65 fat grams for the day) and 2 grams saturated fat (10% of the 20 grams saturated fat for the day).

Determining Your Fat Budget

On average, your total fat intake over the course of a day should be limited to 30% of your total calories. To translate 30% calories from fat to fat grams, take the number of calories you need in a day, multiply by 30% (0.3), then divide by 9.

Daily Calories	Your Daily Fat Budget
1,200	40 grams
1,600	53 grams
1,800	60 grams
2,000	67 grams**

Note: Guidelines on food labels are based on 2,000 calories a day, and the fat grams are rounded to 65.

Breakfast Couscous With Fruit, recipe on page 27

Vegetable Breakfast Pizza,
recipe on page 16

Breakfast & Brunch

Pizza for breakfast? Absolutely. Here you'll find a variety of breakfast dishes—new and familiar favorites—that fit your good-health goals. Pear Spirals, Lentil-Rice Breakfast Patties, Stuffed French Toast, and Breakfast Couscous With Fruit are just a few of your many choices.

TOTAL FAT: 9 g
DAILY VALUE FAT: 14%
SATURATED FAT: 3 g
DAILY VALUE SATURATED FAT: 15%

NUTRITION FACTS
PER SERVING:

Calories	184
Total Fat	9 g
Saturated Fat	3 g
Cholesterol	132 mg
Sodium	217 mg
Carbohydrate	132 g
Fiber	2 g
Protein	12 g

EXCHANGES:
1 Starch
1 Vegetable
1 Lean Meat

START TO FINISH: 18 minutes

Asparagus-Potato Scramble

If you use fresh asparagus, rinse it thoroughly in cold water and snap off the woody ends, finding the spot where the stalks break easily by gently bending them.

Nonstick spray coating
2 cups frozen loose-pack diced hash brown potatoes with onions and peppers, thawed
2 tablespoons sliced green onion (1)
6 beaten egg whites*
3 beaten eggs*
3 tablespoons skim milk
1 tablespoon snipped fresh basil or ½ teaspoon dried basil, crushed
⅛ teaspoon salt
⅛ teaspoon pepper
1 pound asparagus, cut into 1-inch pieces (1½ cups) or one 10-ounce package frozen cut asparagus, thawed and well drained
¼ cup shredded reduced-fat sharp cheddar cheese (1 ounce)

♣ Generously spray an unheated large nonstick skillet with nonstick coating. Preheat over medium heat. Add the hash brown potatoes and green onion; cook and stir over medium heat for for 4 to 5 minutes or until beginning to brown.

♣ Meanwhile, in a large mixing bowl beat together egg whites, whole eggs, milk, basil, salt, and pepper. Stir in asparagus (thawed, if using frozen). Pour egg mixture over potatoes and green onion. Cook, without stirring, until mixture begins to set on the bottom and around edge. Using a spatula or a large spoon, lift and fold the partially cooked egg mixture so the uncooked portion flows underneath. Continue cooking and folding about 4 minutes more or until eggs are cooked through, but are still glossy and moist.

♣ Remove skillet from heat; sprinkle with cheese. Cover and let stand 1 minute or until cheese is melted. Makes 5 servings.

*Note: You can substitute 1½ cups refrigerated or frozen egg product (thawed) instead of the egg whites and whole eggs.

TOTAL FAT: 7 g
DAILY VALUE FAT: 11%
SATURATED FAT: 1 g
DAILY VALUE SATURATED FAT: 5%

NUTRITION FACTS
PER SERVING:

Calories	251
Total Fat	7 g
Saturated Fat	1 g
Cholesterol	7 mg
Sodium	559 mg
Carbohydrate	34 g
Fiber	3 g
Protein	14 g

EXCHANGES:
2 Starch
1 Vegetable
1 Lean Meat

PREPARATION TIME: 20 minutes
BAKING TIME: 8 minutes

Vegetable Breakfast Pizza

America's favorite food just took the a.m. shift. Count on frozen hash browns and an Italian bread shell to get breakfast on the table in short order. (See photograph on pages 12 and 13.)

Nonstick spray coating
1½ cups frozen loose-pack diced hash brown potatoes or country hash browns, with skin, thawed
1 cup sliced fresh mushrooms
½ cup shredded carrot
½ cup shredded zucchini
¼ cup chopped onion
1 cup refrigerated or frozen egg product (thawed) or 4 eggs
¼ cup skim milk
1 16-ounce Italian bread shell (Boboli) (12 inch)
½ cup shredded reduced-fat mozzarella cheese (2 ounces)
½ cup chopped tomato

♣ Spray an unheated large skillet with nonstick coating. Preheat over medium heat. Add potatoes, mushrooms, carrot, zucchini, and onion to skillet. Cook and stir about 3 minutes or until vegetables are tender.

♣ In a small mixing bowl stir together egg product or eggs and milk. Add to skillet. Cook, without stirring, until mixture begins to set on the bottom and around the edge. Using a spatula or a large spoon, lift and fold the partially cooked mixture. Continue cooking and folding until egg product is cooked through, but is still glossy and moist. Remove from heat.

♣ To assemble pizza, place Italian bread shell on a baking sheet or in a 12-inch pizza pan. Sprinkle *half* of the cheese over the shell. Top with egg mixture, tomato, and remaining cheese. Bake in a 375° oven for 8 to 10 minutes or until cheese is melted. Makes 8 servings.

Lentil-Rice Breakfast Patties

Miss that morning sizzle in your skillet? Try boldly flavored lentil-and-rice patties as a tasty substitute for higher-fat sausage.

2¼ cups water
½ cup finely chopped onion
⅓ cup regular brown rice
2 cloves garlic, minced
¾ cup dry lentils, rinsed and drained
1 15-ounce can garbanzo beans, rinsed and drained
¾ cup regular rolled oats
2 slightly beaten egg whites
¾ teaspoon ground sage
½ teaspoon dried savory, crushed
¼ teaspoon salt
⅛ teaspoon ground black pepper
⅛ teaspoon ground red pepper
⅛ teaspoon ground nutmeg
¼ cup finely chopped toasted almonds
   Nonstick spray coating
   Plain fat-free yogurt (optional)

♣ In a 2-quart saucepan combine the water, onion, *uncooked* brown rice, and garlic. Bring to boiling; reduce heat. Simmer, covered, for 20 minutes. Add the lentils. Simmer, covered, about 25 minutes more or until rice and lentils are tender. Remove the saucepan from heat.

♣ Stir garbanzo beans into lentil-rice mixture. Mash with a potato masher. Stir in rolled oats. Let stand for 5 minutes.

♣ In a medium mixing bowl stir together the egg whites, sage, savory, salt, black pepper, red pepper, and nutmeg. Add the lentil-rice mixture. Stir until combined. Stir in almonds. Using about ¼ cup mixture for each, shape mixture into 16 patties about ½ inch thick. (If desired, you can freeze the uncooked patties. Place patties in a single layer in a freezer container. Seal, label, and freeze for up to 3 months. To thaw, place in refrigerator overnight.)

♣ To cook patties, spray an unheated large skillet with nonstick coating. Cook the patties, up to 8 at a time, over medium heat for 7 to 10 minutes or until lightly browned, turning once. To serve, if desired, top with fat-free yogurt. Makes 16 patties.

TOTAL FAT: 2 g
DAILY VALUE FAT: 3%
SATURATED FAT: 0 g
DAILY VALUE SATURATED FAT: 0%

NUTRITION FACTS
PER PATTY:

Calories	102
Total Fat	2 g
Saturated Fat	0 g
Cholesterol	0 mg
Sodium	127 mg
Carbohydrate	16 g
Fiber	2 g
Protein	6 g

EXCHANGES:
1 Starch
½ Fat

PREPARATION TIME: 1 hour 15 minutes
COOKING TIME: 7 minutes

Blueberry-Buttermilk Pancakes
With Orange Sauce

Soak up every bit of the tangy citrus sauce with these berry-stuffed, low-fat pancakes. The easy orange sauce makes a refreshing change from regular pancake syrup.

1 **cup all-purpose flour**
1 **tablespoon sugar**
1 **teaspoon baking powder**
½ **teaspoon baking soda**
⅛ **teaspoon salt**
1 **slightly beaten egg white**
1 **cup buttermilk**
2 **teaspoons cooking oil**
1 **teaspoon vanilla**
¾ **cup fresh or frozen blueberries**
 Orange wedges and/or fresh blueberries
  (optional)
1 **recipc Orange Sauce**

♣ For pancakes, in a medium mixing bowl stir together the flour, sugar, baking powder, baking soda, and salt.

♣ In another mixing bowl stir together the egg white, buttermilk, cooking oil, and vanilla. Add all at once to the flour mixture. Stir just until combined but still slightly lumpy. Gently fold in the blueberries.

♣ For each pancake, pour about ¼ *cup* of the batter onto a hot nonstick griddle. Cook over medium heat about 2 minutes on each side or until pancakes are golden brown, turning to cook second sides when pancakes have bubbly surfaces and slightly dry edges. Serve with Orange Sauce. If desired, garnish with orange wedges and/or additional blueberries. Cover and chill any remaining Orange Sauce. Makes 4 to 5 servings (2 pancakes and 2 tablespoons sauce per serving).

Orange Sauce: In a small saucepan stir together ¼ cup *orange juice concentrate,* 1 tablespoon *sugar,* and 1 tablespoon *cornstarch.* Add 1 cup *water.* Cook and stir over medium heat until thickened and bubbly. Cook and stir sauce for 2 minutes more. Serve warm with pancakes.

TOTAL FAT: 3 g
DAILY VALUE FAT: 5%
SATURATED FAT: 1 g
DAILY VALUE SATURATED FAT: 5%

NUTRITION FACTS
PER SERVING:

Calories	204
Total Fat	3 g
Saturated Fat	1 g
Cholesterol	2 mg
Sodium	396 mg
Carbohydrate	37 g
Fiber	2 g
Protein	6 g

EXCHANGES:
2 Starch
½ Fruit
½ Fat

PREPARATION TIME: 20 minutes
COOKING TIME: 4 minutes

TOTAL FAT: 1 g
DAILY VALUE FAT: 2%
SATURATED FAT: 0 g
DAILY VALUE SATURATED FAT: 0%

NUTRITION FACTS
PER STUFFED SLICE:

Calories	150
Total Fat	1 g
Saturated Fat	0 g
Cholesterol	30 mg
Sodium	163 mg
Carbohydrate	29 g
Fiber	0 g
Protein	7 g

EXCHANGES:
2 Starch

START TO FINISH: 20 minutes

Stuffed French Toast

For a change of taste, top fruit-and-cream cheese-filled French toast with a drizzle of maple syrup or a dusting of powdered sugar instead of the spreadable fruit.

½ cup fat-free cream cheese (about 5 ounces)
2 tablespoons apricot or strawberry spreadable fruit
8 1-inch-thick slices French bread
2 slightly beaten egg whites
1 beaten egg
¾ cup skim milk
½ teaspoon vanilla
⅛ teaspoon apple pie spice
Nonstick spray coating
½ cup apricot or strawberry spreadable fruit
Sliced fresh apricots or strawberries (optional)

♣ In a small bowl stir together cream cheese and the 2 tablespoons spreadable fruit. Using a serrated knife, cut a pocket in each of the bread slices by making a cut in the center of each slice from the top almost to the bottom. Fill each pocket with some of the cream cheese mixture.

♣ In a shallow bowl beat together the egg whites, whole egg, milk, vanilla, and apple pie spice. Spray a nonstick griddle with nonstick coating. Preheat over medium heat.

♣ Dip bread slices into egg white mixture, coating both sides. Cook bread slices about 3 minutes or until golden brown, turning once to cook second sides. Meanwhile, in a small saucepan heat the ½ cup spreadable fruit until melted, stirring frequently. Serve over French toast. If desired, garnish with fresh apricots or strawberries. Makes 8 stuffed slices.

TOTAL FAT: 8 g
DAILY VALUE FAT: 12%
SATURATED FAT: 2 g
DAILY VALUE SATURATED FAT: 10%

NUTRITION FACTS
PER SERVING:

Calories	246
Total Fat	8 g
Saturated Fat	2 g
Cholesterol	3 mg
Sodium	132 mg
Carbohydrate	42 g
Fiber	1 g
Protein	3 g

EXCHANGES:
2 Starch
½ Fruit
1 Fat

PREPARATION TIME: 20 minutes
BAKING TIME: 30 minutes

Apple Streusel Coffee Cake

Delight family and brunch guests with this moist, tender, and full-of-fruit coffee cake, then surprise them with the news that it's low in fat.

Nonstick spray coating
3 tablespoons brown sugar
1 tablespoon all-purpose flour
½ teaspoon apple pie spice
1 tablespoon butter*
¼ cup finely chopped toasted pecans or walnuts
1½ cups all-purpose flour
¾ cup granulated sugar
2 teaspoons baking powder
⅛ teaspoon salt
1 slightly beaten egg white
½ cup apple juice
3 tablespoons cooking oil
2 medium cooking apples, peeled, cored, and sliced

♣ Spray an 8×8×2-inch baking pan with nonstick coating; set aside.

♣ For streusel topping, in a small mixing bowl stir together the brown sugar, the 1 tablespoon flour, and the apple pie spice. Using a pastry blender, cut in butter until crumbly. Stir in pecans or walnuts. Set aside.

♣ For batter, in a medium mixing bowl stir together the 1½ cups flour, the granulated sugar, baking powder, and salt. In another mixing bowl stir together the egg white, apple juice, and cooking oil. Add juice mixture to flour mixture, stirring just until combined.

♣ Arrange the apple slices on the bottom of the prepared baking pan. Pour batter over apples, spreading evenly. Sprinkle with streusel topping.

♣ Bake in a 350° oven about 30 minutes or until a wooden toothpick inserted near the center comes out clean. Serve coffee cake warm. Makes 9 servings.

Note: When making streusels, crumb crusts, crumb toppings, piecrusts, pastries, and shortbreads or other butter cookies, it is best to use butter. Many margarines will not work as well due to the amount of water they contain.

Pineapple-Bran Muffins

Ginger and pineapple-bran muffins, warm from the oven, and a cup of hot tea or coffee—now that's a perfect way to say good morning.

Nonstick spray coating
1½ cups all-purpose flour
⅔ cup whole bran cereal
⅓ cup sugar
2 teaspoons baking powder
⅛ teaspoon salt
⅛ teaspoon ground ginger
1 slightly beaten egg white
1 8-ounce can crushed pineapple
(juice-packed)
½ cup skim milk
3 tablespoons cooking oil
1 to 2 teaspoons sugar

♣ Spray twelve 2½-inch muffin cups with nonstick coating; set aside.

♣ In a medium mixing bowl stir together the flour, bran cereal, the ⅓ cup sugar, the baking powder, salt, and ginger. Make a well in the center of the flour mixture.

♣ In another mixing bowl stir together the egg white, *undrained* pineapple, milk, and cooking oil. Add all at once to the flour mixture. Stir just until mixture is moistened (batter should be lumpy). Spoon batter into prepared muffin cups, filling each ¾ full. Sprinkle muffin tops lightly with the 1 to 2 teaspoons sugar.

♣ Bake in a 375° oven for 20 to 25 minutes or until the tops are golden. Cool in muffin cups on a wire rack for 5 minutes. Remove from cups; serve warm. Makes 12 muffins.

Secrets to Great Muffins

If you have the following problems with your muffins, try our muffin-making tips:

♣ Peaks and tunnels: Avoid mixing the batter too much. When adding liquid to the dry ingredients, stir until the dry ingredients are just moistened. The batter should be lumpy.

♣ Tough muffins: Make sure you thoroughly mix the egg and milk together before adding them to the dry ingredients.

♣ Crumbly muffins: Mix the batter as the recipe directs, usually until the dry ingredients are just moistened. Muffins don't need a lot of mixing.

TOTAL FAT: 4 g
DAILY VALUE FAT: 6%
SATURATED FAT: 1 g
DAILY VALUE SATURATED FAT: 5%

NUTRITION FACTS
PER MUFFIN:

Calories	128
Total Fat	4 g
Saturated Fat	1 g
Cholesterol	0 mg
Sodium	119 mg
Carbohydrate	24 g
Fiber	2 g
Protein	3 g

EXCHANGES:
1½ Starch
½ Fat

PREPARATION TIME: 10 minutes
BAKING TIME: 20 minutes
COOLING TIME: 5 minutes

Whole Wheat Pear Spirals

A sister to the cinnamon roll, these bran-and-wheat spirals boast a luscious pear-cinnamon filling but not the usual sweet roll calories.

½ cup whole bran cereal
⅔ cup pear nectar or white grape juice
¾ cup all-purpose flour
½ cup whole wheat flour
2 tablespoons granulated sugar
1 teaspoon baking powder
⅛ teaspoon salt
3 tablespoons margarine or butter
¾ cup chopped peeled pear
2 tablespoons granulated sugar
⅛ teaspoon ground cinnamon
    Nonstick spray coating
½ cup sifted powdered sugar
2 to 3 teaspoons pear nectar or white
    grape juice

♣ In a small bowl combine the whole bran cereal and pear nectar or white grape juice; let soak for 5 minutes.

♣ Meanwhile, in a medium mixing bowl stir together the all-purpose flour, whole wheat flour, 2 tablespoons granulated sugar, baking powder, and salt. Using a pastry blender, cut in margarine or butter until the mixture resembles coarse crumbs. Add the bran cereal mixture all at once. Stir just until dough clings together. Let dough rest while preparing the filling.

♣ For filling, in a small bowl stir together the chopped pear, the 2 tablespoons granulated sugar, and the cinnamon. Spray a 9×1½-inch round baking pan with nonstick coating; set pan aside.

♣ On a well-floured surface, knead the dough gently for 10 to 12 strokes (dough will be slightly sticky). Roll dough into a 12×8-inch rectangle. Spread filling evenly over dough. Roll up, jelly-roll style, starting from a long side. Seal seam. Slice into 12 equal pieces

♣ Arrange slices, cut-sides up, in the prepared pan. Bake in a 400° oven about 25 minutes or until golden. Cool in pan on a wire rack for 10 minutes. Remove spirals from pan.

♣ Meanwhile, for glaze, combine the powdered sugar and enough of the 2 to 3 teaspoons pear nectar or grape juice to make a glaze of drizzling consistency. Drizzle warm rolls with glaze. Makes 12 spirals.

TOTAL FAT: 3 g
DAILY VALUE FAT: 5%
SATURATED FAT: 1 g
DAILY VALUE SATURATED FAT: 5%

NUTRITION FACTS
PER SPIRAL:

Calories	121
Total Fat	3 g
Saturated Fat	1 g
Cholesterol	0 mg
Sodium	106 mg
Carbohydrate	24 g
Fiber	2 g
Protein	2 g

EXCHANGES:
1½ Starch

PREPARATION TIME: 18 minutes
BAKING TIME: 25 minutes
COOLING TIME: 10 minutes

TOTAL FAT: **4 g**
DAILY VALUE FAT: **6%**
SATURATED FAT: **0 g**
DAILY VALUE SATURATED FAT: **0%**

NUTRITION FACTS
PER SERVING:

Calories	175
Total Fat	4 g
Saturated Fat	0 g
Cholesterol	1 mg
Sodium	686 mg
Carbohydrate	32 g
Fiber	3 g
Protein	5 g

EXCHANGES:
2 Starch
½ Fat

PREPARATION TIME: **5 minutes**
COOKING TIME: **10 minutes**

Fruit & Nut Cereal

Stir together a batch of this cracked wheat cereal mix and store it in the refrigerator. A bowlful cooks quickly and really satisfies on those blustery, cold-weather days.

¾ **cup cornmeal**
½ **cup cracked wheat cereal or bulgur**
½ **cup regular rolled oats**
½ **cup snipped dried apricots or mixed dried fruit bits**
⅓ **cup coarsely chopped walnuts or pecans**
⅛ **teaspoon ground cardamom**
⅛ **teaspoon ground nutmeg**
⅛ **teaspoon ground ginger**

♣ In an airtight storage container stir together the cornmeal, cracked wheat cereal, rolled oats, apricots, walnuts or pecans, cardamom, nutmeg, and ginger. Cover and store in the refrigerator for up to 1 month. Makes 2⅔ cups (8 servings).

To cook 1 serving: In a small saucepan bring 1 cup *water* and a dash *salt* to boiling. Slowly stir in ⅓ *cup* cereal mixture. Simmer, uncovered, about 10 minutes or until desired consistency. Serve topped with *skim milk* and *sugar.*

To cook 2 servings: Prepare as directed for 1 serving, *except* use 2 cups *water* and ⅛ teaspoon *salt* with ⅔ *cup* cereal mixture.

Waves of Grain

Looking for a rice alternative? Try some wheat products. The cereal recipe above calls for either cracked wheat or bulgur. Look for these products in a health food store or check your grocer's shelves next to the hot cereals or flour. Here's the difference between the two:

Cracked wheat is the whole, unprocessed kernel of the wheat berry broken into various sizes of pieces (fine, medium, or coarse). Add cracked wheat to baked goods or casseroles (before baking or cooking) for a nutty flavor and crunchy texture.

Bulgur is a wheat berry that has had the bran removed. It is then steamed, dried, and also ground into fine, medium, or coarse pieces. Because bulgur is precooked, it cooks quickly or needs only a brief soaking before using.

Breakfast Couscous With Fruit

Take a break from the usual bowl of flakes and try this tart-sweet couscous and fruit medley. It's like having a bowl of rice pudding for breakfast. (See photograph on page 12.)

1   cup rice-based nondairy beverage or
     skim milk
¼   teaspoon ground cinnamon
     Dash ground nutmeg
1   cup couscous
⅓   cup orange juice
¾   cup cranberries
2   tablespoons water
2   tablespoons honey
1   11-ounce can mandarin orange sections,
     drained
2   tablespoons toasted slivered almonds

♣ In a medium saucepan combine nondairy beverage or skim milk, cinnamon, and nutmeg. Bring to boiling over medium heat. Add couscous. Cover and remove from heat. Let stand for 5 minutes. Stir in orange juice. Fluff with a fork.

♣ Meanwhile, in a small saucepan combine cranberries, water, and honey. Cook over low heat for 4 to 5 minutes or until the cranberry skins begin to pop. Remove from heat. Gently stir in mandarin oranges.

♣ To serve, spoon couscous mixture into serving bowls. Top with warm cranberry-orange mixture and sprinkle with almonds. Makes 4 servings.

No-Milk Milk

When you think of milk, you most likely think of the kind that comes from a cow. People who have an intolerance to milk or who are vegetarian may avoid drinking cow's milk. But there are other options, such as Rice Dream, a milk substitute made from organic brown rice. Unlike cow's milk, rice milk does not naturally contain calcium. Nor does rice milk contain vitamins A and D. But it is available enriched with all three. Rice milk is low in fat and there's no cholesterol. Look for rice milk in health food stores or next to canned milk in your supermarket in a 32-ounce, shelf-stable box. Its pleasant flavor may surprise you.

TOTAL FAT: 3 g
DAILY VALUE FAT: 5%
SATURATED FAT: 0 g
DAILY VALUE SATURATED FAT: 0%

NUTRITION FACTS
PER SERVING:

Calories	312
Total Fat	3 g
Saturated Fat	0 g
Cholesterol	0 mg
Sodium	11 mg
Carbohydrate	66 g
Fiber	8 g
Protein	8 g

EXCHANGES:
2½ Starch
1½ Fruit

START TO FINISH: 15 minutes

Mini Spinach Calzones, recipe on page 38

Layered Southwestern Dip,
recipe on page 30

Snacks & Appetizers

Snacks and appetizers can be part of a healthful diet—especially when you choose wisely. All of the health-conscious recipes in this chapter, including Gorgonzola and Onion Tart, Layered Southwestern Dip, Bruschetta, Apple-Cranberry Fruit Dip, and Vegetable Nachos, will meet your snack or party needs.

TOTAL FAT: 2 g
DAILY VALUE FAT: 3%
SATURATED FAT: 1 g
DAILY VALUE SATURATED FAT: 5%

NUTRITION FACTS
PER SERVING:

Calories	80
Total Fat	2 g
Saturated Fat	1 g
Cholesterol	2 mg
Sodium	178 mg
Carbohydrate	12 g
Fiber	1 g
Protein	3 g

EXCHANGES:
1 Starch

Layered Southwestern Dip:
PREPARATION TIME: 20 minutes

Homemade Tortilla Chips:
PPREAPRATION TIME: 10 minutes
BAKING TIME: 10 minutes (per batch)

Layered Southwestern Dip

If you want a real crowd pleaser, seven layers of fresh, colorful Mexican flavors will do the trick. When you have the time, make your own low-fat chips. (See photograph on pages 28 and 29.)

 2 cups shredded lettuce
 1 15-ounce can reduced-sodium black
      beans, rinsed and drained
 ½ cup chopped green sweet pepper
 2 tablespoons bottled chopped red
      jalapeño peppers or canned diced
      green chili peppers
 1 8-ounce carton fat-free dairy sour cream
 1 8-ounce jar chunky salsa
 ½ cup shredded reduced-fat cheddar cheese
      (2 ounces)
 2 tablespoons chopped pitted ripe olives
 1 recipe Homemade Tortilla Chips

♣ Line a 12-inch platter with the shredded lettuce. In a small bowl stir together the black beans, green sweet pepper, and jalapeño peppers or green chili peppers. Spoon over lettuce, leaving a lettuce border. Spoon sour cream over bean mixture; gently spread in a smooth layer, leaving a border of bean mixture.

♣ Drain excess liquid from salsa. Spoon salsa over sour cream layer, leaving a border of sour cream. Sprinkle cheese over salsa. Top with olives. Serve immediately. (Or, cover and chill for up to 6 hours.) Serve with Homemade Tortilla Chips. Makes 24 appetizer servings.

Homemade Tortilla Chips: Cut sixteen 7- to 8-inch *flour tortillas* into 6 wedges each. Arrange wedges in a single layer on ungreased baking sheets. Bake in a 350° oven for 10 to 15 minutes or until dry and crisp. Makes 96.

White Bean & Pine Nut Dip

Similar in consistency to hummus or Mexican bean dip, this easy blender dip has a nutty, herb flavor all its own.

¼ cup soft bread crumbs
2 tablespoons dry white wine or vegetable broth
1 15-ounce can white kidney beans (cannellini) or great Northern beans, rinsed and drained
¼ cup fat-free dairy sour cream French onion dip
3 tablespoons toasted pine nuts
⅛ teaspoon ground red pepper
2 teaspoons snipped fresh oregano or basil or ½ teaspoon dried oregano or basil, crushed
1 large red, yellow, or green sweet pepper (optional)
 Snipped fresh chives (optional)
1 recipe Toasted Pita Chips

♣ In a small mixing bowl combine the bread crumbs and wine or vegetable broth. Let stand for 5 minutes.

♣ Meanwhile, in a blender container or food processor bowl combine beans, sour cream dip, pine nuts, and ground red pepper. Cover and blend or process until almost smooth. Add bread crumb mixture. Cover and blend or process until smooth. Stir in the oregano or basil. Cover and chill for 2 to 24 hours to blend flavors.

♣ To serve in pepper shell, place sweet pepper on its side; slice off the top one-third of the pepper and reserve. Remove seeds and membranes from remaining pepper piece, leaving pepper whole, creating a boat. Spoon bean mixture into pepper shell. If desired, finely chop reserved pepper piece. Sprinkle chopped pepper and chives over dip. Serve with Toasted Pita Chips. Makes 12 appetizer servings (1½ cups).

Toasted Pita Chips: Split 5 large *pita bread rounds* in half horizontally. Using a knife, cut each pita round half into 6 wedges. Arrange wedges in a single layer on ungreased baking sheets. Spray pita wedges with *nonstick spray coating*. Lightly sprinkle with *paprika*. Bake in a 350° oven for 12 to 15 minutes or until wedges are crisp and golden. Makes 60 chips.

TOTAL FAT: **2 g**
DAILY VALUE FAT: **3%**
SATURATED FAT: **0 g**
DAILY VALUE SATURATED FAT: **0%**

NUTRITION FACTS PER SERVING:

Calories	111
Total Fat	2 g
Saturated Fat	0 g
Cholesterol	0 mg
Sodium	197 mg
Carbohydrate	20 g
Fiber	2 g
Protein	5 g

EXCHANGES:
1½ Starch

White Bean and Pine Nut Dip:
PREPARATION TIME: **15 minutes**
CHILLING TIME: **2 hours**

Toasted Pita Chips:
PREPARATION TIME: **5 minutes**
BAKING TIME: **12 minutes (per batch)**

TOTAL FAT: 7 g
DAILY VALUE FAT: 11%
SATURATED FAT: 2 g
DAILY VALUE SATURATED FAT: 10%

**NUTRITION FACTS
PER SERVING:**

Calories	234
Total Fat	7 g
Saturated Fat	2
Cholesterol	7 mg
Sodium	498 mg
Carbohydrate	32 g
Fiber	4 g
Protein	10 g

EXCHANGES:
2 Starch
1 Vegetable
1 Fat

PREPARATION TIME: 20 minutes
BAKING TIME: 5 minutes

Vegetable Nachos

An old Tex-Mex snack favorite takes on a bold, new look and flavor when you pile tortilla chips high with fresh vegetables, pinto beans, and cilantro sour cream.

½ cup fat-free dairy sour cream
1 tablespoon finely snipped fresh cilantro
1 tablespoon cooking oil
1 small zucchini, quartered lengthwise and thinly sliced (about 1 cup)
1 medium red or yellow onion, chopped (½ cup)
½ cup shredded carrot
1½ teaspoons ground cumin
1 15-ounce can pinto beans, rinsed and drained
1 recipe Homemade Tortilla Chips (see page 30)
1 4-ounce can diced green chili peppers, drained
½ cup seeded and chopped tomato
¾ cup shredded reduced-fat cheddar cheese (3 ounces)
　Fresh cilantro (optional)
　Salsa (optional)

♣ In a small mixing bowl stir together sour cream and cilantro; cover and chill.

♣ In a large skillet cook zucchini, onion, carrot, and cumin in hot oil over medium heat for 3 to 4 minutes or until vegetables are crisp-tender. Stir in pinto beans.

♣ Arrange Homemade Tortilla Chips on an 11- or 12-inch ovenproof platter or on a baking sheet. Spoon the bean mixture onto the chips. Sprinkle with chili peppers, tomato, and cheese. Bake in a 350° oven for 5 to 7 minutes or until cheese is melted.

♣ To serve, transfer nachos to a serving platter. If desired, garnish with cilantro. Pass the sour cream mixture and, if desired, the salsa. Makes 8 appetizer servings.

TOTAL FAT: 3 g
DAILY VALUE FAT: 5%
SATURATED FAT: 1 g
DAILY VALUE SATURATED FAT: 5%

NUTRITION FACTS
PER TRIANGLE:

Calories	66
Total Fat	3 g
Saturated Fat	1 g
Cholesterol	7 mg
Sodium	85 mg
Carbohydrate	9 g
Fiber	0 g
Protein	2 g

EXCHANGES:
½ Starch
½ Fat

PREPARATION TIME: 25 minutes
BAKING TIME: 15 minutes

Golden Phyllo Triangles

Your guests will thank you for these flaky, cream-cheese-stuffed pastry appetizers that are actually low in fat. As a bonus, you can fix them ahead and freeze them.

1 8-ounce package reduced-fat cream cheese (Neufchâtel), softened
1 egg white
⅓ cup coarsely shredded carrot
¼ cup finely chopped green sweet pepper
⅛ teaspoon ground red pepper
8 sheets frozen phyllo dough, thawed (18×14-inch sheets)
   Nonstick spray coating
1 recipe Apricot Dipping Sauce

♣ For filling, in a medium mixing bowl stir together cream cheese, egg white, carrot, green pepper, and ground red pepper.

♣ Lightly spray 1 sheet of phyllo dough with nonstick coating. Place another sheet of phyllo dough on top of the first sheet. Spray with nonstick coating. Cover remaining phyllo with plastic wrap; set aside.

♣ Cut the 2-layered phyllo sheets lengthwise into 6 equal strips. For each triangle, spoon about 2 teaspoons of filling about 1 inch from one end of the strip. Starting at the same end, fold 1 of the points over the filling so it lines up with other side of the strip, forming a triangle. Continue folding each strip like a flag into a triangular shape. Repeat with remaining strips.

♣ Repeat 3 more times with the remaining sheets of phyllo dough, spray coating, and filling. (If desired, place unbaked triangles in a covered freezer container and freeze for up to 2 months.)

♣ To bake, place triangles (if frozen, do not thaw) on a baking sheet; lightly spray the tops of the triangles with nonstick coating. Bake triangles in a 375° oven about 15 minutes or until golden. Serve warm with Apricot Dipping Sauce. Makes 24 triangles.

Apricot Dipping Sauce: In a small saucepan combine ½ cup *apricot preserves,* 1 tablespoon thinly sliced *green onion,* 1 tablespoon *bottled hoisin sauce,* and ⅛ teaspoon *ground ginger.* Heat and stir until preserves are melted.

Potato Skins With Roasted Pepper

All-American yes, but these crispy potato skins take an Italian twist with roasted red peppers and Italian seasonings.

6 medium baking potatoes (about 2 pounds total)
  Ground black pepper
1 7-ounce jar roasted red sweet peppers, drained and chopped
3 tablespoons thinly sliced green onions
1 cup shredded reduced-fat mozzarella cheese (4 ounces)
½ cup light dairy sour cream
¼ teaspoon dried Italian seasoning, crushed
  Sliced green onions (optional)

♣ Scrub potatoes thoroughly and prick with a fork. Bake in a 425° oven for 40 to 45 minutes or until tender; cool.

♣ Halve each potato lengthwise. Scoop out the inside of each potato half, leaving a shell about ¼ inch thick. Cover and chill the scooped out potato for another use.

♣ Line a 15×10×1-inch baking pan with foil. Arrange potato halves, cut sides up, on baking sheet. Sprinkle with black pepper. Sprinkle roasted red peppers and the 3 tablespoons green onions evenly over potato halves. Top with mozzarella cheese. (If desired, cover and chill for up to 24 hours before baking.)

♣ Bake skins in a 450° oven for 8 to 10 minutes or until cheese is melted and potato pieces are heated through. Meanwhile, stir together the sour cream and Italian seasoning. If desired, sprinkle potato skins with additional green onions. Serve warm with sour cream mixture. Makes 12 appetizer servings.

TOTAL FAT: 2 g
DAILY VALUE FAT: 3%
SATURATED FAT: 1 g
DAILY VALUE SATURATED FAT: 5%

NUTRITION FACTS PER SERVING:

Calories	90
Total Fat	2 g
Saturated Fat	1 g
Cholesterol	6 mg
Sodium	84 mg
Carbohydrate	13 g
Fiber	1 g
Protein	4 g

EXCHANGES:
1 Starch

PREPARATION TIME: 20 minutes
BAKING TIME: 48 minutes

Bruschetta

Assemble pesto-topped bruschetta minutes before serving. Toast the bread slices the day before and make the spinach pesto a day or two in advance.

- 1 **8-ounce loaf baguette-style French bread**
  Nonstick spray coating
- 1½ **cups firmly packed torn fresh spinach**
- ¼ **cup grated Parmesan cheese**
- 3 **tablespoons almonds**
- 3 **tablespoons snipped fresh basil or**
  1 tablespoon dried basil, crushed
- 1 **large clove garlic, quartered**
- ⅛ **teaspoon salt**
- 2 **tablespoons olive oil**
- 2 **tablespoons water**
- 1 **cup chopped red and/or yellow tomato**
- 2 **tablespoons thinly sliced green onion**
- 2 **teaspoons olive oil**
- ⅛ **teaspoon pepper**
  Fresh basil (optional)

♣ For the toasts, cut bread into ½-inch-thick slices. Spray both sides of each slice lightly with nonstick coating. Place on an ungreased baking sheet. Bake in a 425° oven about 5 minutes or until crisp and lightly browned, turning once. (If desired, transfer the cooled toasts to a storage container. Cover and store the toasts at room temperature for up to 24 hours.)

♣ For pesto, in a blender container or food processor bowl combine the spinach, Parmesan cheese, almonds, basil, garlic, and salt. Cover and blend or process with several on-off turns until a paste forms, stopping the machine several times and scraping the sides. With machine running, gradually add the 2 tablespoons olive oil and the water, blending or processing until the mixture is the consistency of soft butter. (If desired, cover and chill the pesto for up to 2 days.)

♣ For the tomato topper, in a small bowl stir together chopped tomato, green onion, the 2 teaspoons olive oil, and the pepper.

♣ To assemble, spread each toast with a thin layer of pesto; top each with some of the tomato topper. If desired, garnish with fresh basil. Makes 18 to 20 slices.

TOTAL FAT: 4 g
DAILY VALUE FAT: 6%
SATURATED FAT: 1 g
DAILY VALUE SATURATED FAT: 5%

NUTRITION FACTS
PER SERVING:

Calories	70
Total Fat	4 g
Saturated Fat	1 g
Cholesterol	1 mg
Sodium	122 mg
Carbohydrate	8 g
Fiber	0 g
Protein	2 g

EXCHANGES:
½ **Starch**
½ **Fat**

PREPARATION TIME: 20 minutes
BAKING TIME: 5 minutes

TOTAL FAT: 2 g
DAILY VALUE FAT: 3%
SATURATED FAT: 1 g
DAILY VALUE SATURATED FAT: 5%

NUTRITION FACTS
PER CALZONE:

Calories	38
Total Fat	2 g
Saturated Fat	1 g
Cholesterol	4 mg
Sodium	63 mg
Carbohydrate	5 g
Fiber	0 g
Protein	1 g

EXCHANGES:
½ Starch

PREPARATION TIME: 30 minutes
BAKING TIME: 8 minutes
COOLING TIME: 5 minutes

Mini Spinach Calzones

Using refrigerated pizza dough takes the work out of these pizza pockets, while spinach and reduced-fat cream cheese keep them good for you. (Pictured on pages 28 and 29.)

½ of a 10-ounce package frozen chopped spinach, thawed and well-drained
½ of an 8-ounce package reduced-fat cream cheese (Neufchâtel), softened
2 tablespoons finely chopped green onion
1 tablespoon grated Parmesan cheese
   Dash pepper
1 10-ounce package refrigerated pizza dough
   Water
1 tablespoon milk
   Light spaghetti sauce (optional)

♣ For filling, in a small mixing bowl stir together the spinach, cream cheese, green onion, Parmesan cheese, and pepper. Set aside.

♣ Unroll pizza dough. On a lightly floured surface, roll dough into a 15-inch square. Using a knife, cut into twenty-five 3-inch squares. Spoon a rounded teaspoon of filling onto each dough square. Brush edges of each square with water. Lift a corner of each square and stretch dough over the filling to the opposite corner, making a triangle. Press edges of the dough well with fingers or a fork to seal.

♣ Line a baking sheet with foil; lightly grease the foil. Arrange the calzones on the baking sheet. Prick tops of calzones with a fork. Brush milk over the calzones. Bake in a 425° oven for 8 to 10 minutes or until golden. Let stand for 5 minutes before serving. If desired, serve with light spaghetti sauce. Makes 25 calzones.

Greek-Style Stuffed
Mushrooms

Perk up any appetizer buffet or antipasto tray with these tempting mushrooms brimming with broccoli, feta cheese, garlic, and oregano.

20 large fresh mushrooms, 1½ to 2 inches in diameter (about 1½ pounds)
1 cup finely chopped broccoli
1 medium onion, chopped (½ cup)
2 tablespoons fine dry bread crumbs
2 tablespoons crumbled feta cheese
2 cloves garlic, minced
½ teaspoon dried oregano, crushed
⅛ teaspoon salt
⅛ teaspoon pepper
Nonstick spray coating

♣ Clean mushrooms. Remove stems from mushrooms. Set caps aside. Chop enough mushroom stems to make 1 cup.

♣ In a medium saucepan cook broccoli, onion, and the chopped mushroom stems in a small amount of *boiling water* for 4 to 5 minutes or until just tender. Drain well. Stir in bread crumbs, feta cheese, garlic, oregano, salt, and pepper. Spray a 15×10×1-inch baking pan with nonstick coating.

♣ Spoon the crumb mixture into mushroom caps. Place the stuffed mushroom caps in the prepared baking pan. Bake mushrooms, uncovered, in a 425° oven for 10 to 15 minutes or until mushrooms are tender and heated through. Makes 20 mushrooms.

Minding Your Mushrooms

When shopping for fresh mushrooms, look for those that are firm, fresh, and plump with no bruising or moistness. If they're spotted or slimy, don't buy them.

Store mushrooms, unwashed, in the refrigerator for up to 2 days. If they are prepackaged, store them in their original packaging. Don't store mushrooms in a closed plastic bag; mushrooms need to breathe. Store loose unpackaged mushrooms in a paper bag or damp cloth bag in the refrigerator.

Clean mushrooms with a damp, clean cloth for the best results. If you choose to rinse store-bought mushrooms, do it lightly then dry the mushrooms gently with paper towels. Never soak mushrooms; they will absorb too much water and will water out during cooking.

TOTAL FAT: **1 g**
DAILY VALUE FAT: **2%**
SATURATED FAT: **0 g**
DAILY VALUE SATURATED FAT: **0%**

NUTRITION FACTS PER MUSHROOM:

Calories	19
Total Fat	1 g
Saturated Fat	0 g
Cholesterol	1 mg
Sodium	38 mg
Carbohydrate	3 g
Fiber	1 g
Protein	1 g

EXCHANGES:
Free Food

PREPARATION TIME: **25 minutes**
BAKING TIME: **10 minutes**

TOTAL FAT: 4 g
DAILY VALUE FAT: 6%
SATURATED FAT: 1 g
DAILY VALUE SATURATED FAT: 5%

NUTRITION FACTS
PER SERVING:

Calories	85
Total Fat	4 g
Saturated Fat	1 g
Cholesterol	17 mg
Sodium	109 mg
Carbohydrate	9 g
Fiber	0 g
Protein	3 g

EXCHANGES:
½ Starch
1 Vegetable
½ Fat

PREPARATION TIME: 20 minutes
BAKING TIME: 30 minutes

Gorgonzola & Onion Tart

A lower-fat oil pastry and skim milk rather than cream move this scrumptious tart off the list of the forbidden and onto the list of low-fat and luscious.

Nonstick spray coating
1¼ cups all-purpose flour
½ teaspoon dried thyme, chervil, or
　　marjoram leaves, crushed
¼ teaspoon salt
¼ cup skim milk
3 tablespoons cooking oil
1 cup thinly sliced onion
½ cup shredded zucchini
½ cup crumbled Gorgonzola or blue cheese
　　(2 ounces)
2 egg whites
1 egg
¼ teaspoon pepper
½ cup skim milk
　　Fresh thyme, chervil, or marjoram
　　(optional)
　　Pear or apple slices (optional)

♣ Spray a 9-inch tart pan with removable sides with nonstick coating. Set aside.

♣ For pastry, in a medium mixing bowl stir together the flour, desired dried herb, and salt. In a 1-cup measure combine ¼ cup milk and oil. Add milk mixture all at once to flour mixture. Stir lightly with a fork. On lightly floured surface, flatten the ball with your hands. Roll dough from center to the edge, forming a circle about 11 inches in diameter. Ease pastry into prepared tart pan, being careful not to stretch the pastry. Trim the pastry even with the edge of the tart pan. Do not prick pastry. Line pastry shell with a double thickness of heavy-duty foil. Press down firmly but gently. Bake in a 425° oven for 5 minutes. Remove foil. Bake for 5 to 7 minutes more or until the pastry is nearly done. Remove from the oven and place on a wire rack. Reduce the oven temperature to 375°.

♣ Meanwhile, for filling, cook onion and zucchini in a small amount of *boiling water* about 5 minutes or until onion is tender. Drain well. In a medium mixing bowl beat the Gorgonzola or blue cheese, egg whites, whole egg, and pepper with an electric mixer on low speed until combined. (Cheese will be lumpy.) Stir in onion mixture and the ½ cup skim milk.

♣ Spoon filling into prebaked pastry. Bake in 375° oven about 20 minutes or until a knife inserted near the center comes out clean. Cool on a wire rack for 15 minutes. Carefully remove sides of tart pan. Serve warm. If desired, garnish with fresh herb and pear or apple slices. Makes 16 appetizer servings.

TOTAL FAT: 0 g

DAILY VALUE FAT: 0%

SATURATED FAT: 0 g

DAILY VALUE SATURATED FAT: 0%

NUTRITION FACTS

PER SERVING AND ½ OF

AN APPLE:

Calories	66
Total Fat	0 g
Saturated Fat	0 g
Cholesterol	1 mg
Sodium	14 mg
Carbohydrate	15 g
Fiber	2 g
Protein	1 g

EXCHANGES:

1 Fruit

PREPARATION TIME: 20 minutes

STANDING TIME: 1 hour

CHILLING TIME: 2 hours

Apple-Cranberry Fruit Dip

Enticing as an appetizer, elegant as dessert. Use this fruity dip as a sauce over slices of angel food cake or as a filling for cream puffs.

¾ cup apple-cranberry juice cocktail
2 teaspoons cornstarch
1 8-ounce carton vanilla low-fat yogurt
Assorted fruit dippers, such as apple or pear slices, pineapple chunks, melon balls, whole strawberries, or kiwifruit slices

♣ In a small saucepan combine apple-cranberry juice cocktail and cornstarch. Cook and stir over medium heat until mixture is thickened and bubbly. Cook and stir for 2 minutes more. Remove from heat; cool.

♣ Stir the vanilla yogurt into the cooled mixture. Transfer to a serving bowl. Cover with plastic wrap and chill for 2 to 24 hours. Serve with fruit dippers. Makes about ten 2-tablespoon servings (1⅓ cups).

Keep the Color

When certain types of fruit, such as apples, pears, peaches, or nectarines, are cut and the flesh is exposed to the air, the fruit's flesh turns brown. But it's easy to avoid this unattractive change in color. After cutting the fruit, immediately submerge the sliced or cut fruit in a bowl of water and lemon juice. A tablespoon of lemon juice per each cup of water will do the trick. Blot the fruit dry with a paper towel just before arranging the fruit on your serving platter.

Strawberries & "Cream"

Balsamic vinegar, with its sweet pungent flavor, ages in wooden barrels for many years. Even though only a little is called for in this recipe, don't be tempted to substitute regular vinegar. The balsamic is what gives this dessert its interesting flavor.

½ of a 15-ounce container low-fat ricotta cheese
1 tablespoon honey
½ teaspoon finely shredded orange peel
2 cups sliced strawberries
2 tablespoons sugar
1 teaspoon balsamic vinegar
Orange curls (optional)

♣ In a blender container or food processor bowl, place ricotta cheese, honey, and orange peel. Cover and blend or process until smooth. Transfer cheese mixture to a bowl. Cover and chill for up to 24 hours.

♣ For berries, in a small bowl combine strawberries and sugar. Let stand at room temperature for 1 hour or until a syrup forms.

♣ To serve, add the vinegar to the strawberries, tossing to combine. Divide berries and syrup among 4 dessert dishes. Top with chilled cheese mixture. If desired, garnish with an orange curl. Makes 4 servings.

Sugar: White Gold

That sweet stuff we call sugar was once so scarce that only the well-to-do could afford such a luxury. That's why it was known as "white gold." Today anyone can buy sugar in any supermarket and at a reasonable price. It is available in a variety of forms, too. But don't be fooled into thinking other sweeteners, such as honey, maple syrup, or corn syrup, are better for you than ordinary table sugar. Nutritionally speaking, they are all pretty much the same. Besides, you shouldn't look to sugar for garnering high nutrition points. In a healthful diet, sugar still should be considered a luxury and be eaten in moderation.

TOTAL FAT: 5 g
DAILY VALUE FAT: 8%
SATURATED FAT: 3 g
DAILY VALUE SATURATED FAT: 15%

**NUTRITION FACTS
PER SERVING:**

Calories	139
Total Fat	5 g
Saturated Fat	3 g
Cholesterol	16 mg
Sodium	68 mg
Carbohydrate	20 g
Fiber	1 g
Protein	7 g

EXCHANGES:
1 Fruit
1 Lean Meat

PREPARATION TIME: 15 minutes
STANDING TIME: 1 hour
CHILLING TIME: up to 24 hours

Six-Bean Salad, recipe on page 46

Tortellini-Vegetable Salad,
recipe on page 58

Star Salads

Salads, such as this Tortellini-Vegetable Salad or Six-Bean Salad, make great main dishes and usually toss together fast. For a lighter meal, select from this inspiring collection of salads that includes Roasted Hot Potato Salad, Taco Salad, and Wild Rice Salad.

TOTAL FAT: 8 g
DAILY VALUE FAT: 12%
SATURATED FAT: 1 g
DAILY VALUE SATURATED FAT: 5%

NUTRITION FACTS
PER SERVING:

Calories	290
Total Fat	8 g
Saturated Fat	1 g
Cholesterol	0 mg
Sodium	498 mg
Carbohydrate	43 g
Fiber	9 g
Protein	13 g

EXCHANGES:
2½ Starch
1 Vegetable
1 Lean Meat
½ Fat

PREPARATION TIME: 20 minutes
CHILLING TIME: 4 hours

Six-Bean Salad

If you haven't tried chipotle chili peppers, here's your chance. They're actually just jalapeño peppers that have been dried and smoked, lending a unique smoky-sweet flavor to dishes. Here they update a long-time favorite, six-bean salad. (Pictured on page 44.)

1 cup frozen cut green beans
1 small dried chipotle chili pepper, crumbled, or ½ to 1 teaspoon crushed red pepper
1 15¼- or 16-ounce can lima beans, rinsed and drained
1 15-ounce can reduced-sodium black beans, rinsed and drained
1 15-ounce can reduced-sodium kidney beans, rinsed and drained
1 15-ounce can reduced-sodium garbanzo beans, rinsed and drained
1 15-ounce can pinto beans, rinsed and drained
2 medium tomatoes, seeded and chopped
¼ cup finely chopped red onion
¼ cup finely chopped green sweet pepper
¼ cup salad oil
¼ teaspoon grated lemon peel
¼ cup lemon juice
1 tablespoon sugar
  Leaf lettuce (optional)

♣ Cook the frozen beans and the crumbled chipotle chili pepper or crushed red pepper according to the bean package directions; drain. Meanwhile, in a large bowl combine lima beans, black beans, kidney beans, garbanzo beans, pinto beans, tomatoes, red onion, and sweet pepper. Stir in the drained green beans; set aside.

♣ For dressing, in a screw-top jar combine the salad oil, lemon peel, lemon juice, and sugar. Cover and shake well. Pour the dressing over bean mixture, tossing to coat. Cover and chill for 4 to 24 hours, stirring once or twice. (The salad may be stored in the refrigerator for up to 3 days). If desired, serve salad on lettuce-lined plates. Makes 8 main-dish servings.

Taco Salad

Stir the leftover canned black beans into your next batch of chili or vegetable soup or mix them with some salsa and fresh cilantro for a healthful baked potato topper.

1 15- or 15½-ounce can navy or great northern beans, rinsed and drained
½ of a 15-ounce can reduced-sodium black beans, rinsed and drained
¾ cup salsa
1 teaspoon chili powder
½ teaspoon garlic powder
6 cups shredded iceberg or leaf lettuce
2 medium tomatoes, chopped
1 cup chopped green sweet pepper
¼ cup shredded reduced-fat cheddar cheese (1 ounce)
¼ cup sliced pitted ripe olives (optional)
1 cup baked tortilla chips
Fat-free dairy sour cream (optional)

♣ For topping, in a medium saucepan stir together the navy or great northern beans, black beans, salsa, chili powder, and garlic powder. Cook over medium heat until heated through, stirring occasionally.

♣ Meanwhile, divide the shredded lettuce among 4 serving plates. Top with bean mixture, tomatoes, sweet pepper, cheese, and olives (if desired). Garnish salads with chips. If desired, top each salad with a spoonful of sour cream. Makes 4 main-dish servings.

TOTAL FAT: 3 g
DAILY VALUE FAT: 5%
SATURATED FAT: 1 g
DAILY VALUE SATURATED FAT: 5%

NUTRITION FACTS PER SERVING:

Calories	264
Total Fat	3 g
Saturated Fat	1 g
Cholesterol	5 mg
Sodium	797 mg
Carbohydrate	43 g
Fiber	5 g
Protein	15 g

EXCHANGES:
2 Starch
2 Vegetable
1 Lean Meat

START TO FINISH: 20 minutes

Hills of Beans

Beans may just be a "perfect food." Here are some reasons why:

♣ Beans come in a huge variety, from large fava beans to burgundy-mottled cranberry beans.

♣ Compared to meat, beans win hands-down for length of storage. Dried beans can be stored at room temperature for up to a year or in your freezer indefinitely. (Imagine eating a T-bone steak from your freezer after about 5 years.)

♣ You can't beat the versatility of beans. Use them in soups, salads, casseroles, and even dips (hummus is made from mashed garbanzo beans, and everyone probably knows about Mexican bean dips).

♣ Beans are cheap, especially compared to other protein sources, such as beef.

♣ Beans are nutrition gold mines. For example, a cup of cooked great northern beans has a whopping 15 grams protein, 6 grams fiber, no cholesterol, and only a trace of fat.

TOTAL FAT: 7 g
DAILY VALUE FAT: 11%
SATURATED FAT: 2 g
DAILY VALUE SATURATED FAT: 10%

**NUTRITION FACTS
PER SERVING:**

Calories	265
Total Fat	7 g
Saturated Fat	2 g
Cholesterol	4 mg
Sodium	782 mg
Carbohydrate	40 g
Fiber	1 g
Protein	13 g

EXCHANGES:

2 Starch
1 Vegetable
1 Lean Meat
½ Fat

PREPARATION TIME: 15 minutes
CHILLING TIME: 4 hours
Croutons:
BAKING TIME: 5 minutes

Blue Cheese & Bean Salad

The homemade croutons make this salad special. If you like, you can substitute other cheeses for the blue cheese, such as goat cheese or freshly shredded Parmesan cheese.

2 15-ounce cans navy beans, rinsed and drained
1 small zucchini, quartered lengthwise and cut into ¼-inch slices (1 cup)
2 small tomatoes, seeded and coarsely chopped (⅔ cup)
2 green onions, thinly sliced (¼ cup)
⅓ cup white wine vinegar
2 tablespoons olive oil
¼ teaspoon dried Italian seasoning, crushed
⅛ teaspoon pepper
2 cups French bread cut into ¾-inch cubes
    Butter-flavored nonstick spray coating
½ teaspoon onion powder
½ teaspoon garlic powder
¼ cup crumbled blue cheese (1 ounce)

♣ In a large mixing bowl combine the navy beans, zucchini, tomatoes, and green onions.

♣ For dressing, in a screw-top jar combine the vinegar, olive oil, Italian seasoning, and pepper. Cover and shake well. Pour dressing over bean mixture, tossing to coat. Cover and chill for 4 to 24 hours, stirring once or twice.

♣ For croutons, before serving salad, arrange bread cubes in a single layer in a 15×10×1-inch baking pan. Spray bread cubes with nonstick coating; toss to coat. Sprinkle with onion powder and garlic powder; toss. Bake in a 350° oven for 5 to 7 minutes or until golden brown, stirring twice. Add the croutons and blue cheese to the bean mixture; toss gently. Serve immediately. Makes 6 main-dish servings.

TOTAL FAT: 3 g
DAILY VALUE FAT: 5%
SATURATED FAT: 1 g
DAILY VALUE SATURATED FAT: 5%

NUTRITION FACTS
PER SERVING:

Calories	270
Total Fat	3 g
Saturated Fat	1 g
Cholesterol	4 mg
Sodium	560 mg
Carbohydrate	49 g
Fiber	2 g
Protein	16 g

EXCHANGES:
2½ Starch
1 Vegetable
1 Lean Meat

PREPARATION TIME: 40 minutes
CHILLING TIME: 4 hours

Creamy Lentil-Corn Salad

Mexican cooks rely on jicama to add texture to many of their dishes. In this salad, the crisp tuber acts as a refreshing counterpoint to the soft lentils. Jicama looks like a large, pale-brown turnip. Look for it year-round in the produce section of larger supermarkets or in Mexican specialty stores.

2½ cups water
 1 cup dry lentils
 ¼ cup chopped onion
 ¼ teaspoon salt
 1 cup frozen whole kernel corn
 ¾ cup coarsely chopped, peeled jicama
 ½ cup light dairy sour cream
 ½ cup fat-free mayonnaise dressing or
       salad dressing
 2 tablespoons snipped fresh basil or
       1 teaspoon dried basil, crushed
 2 tablespoons skim milk (optional)
 1 medium tomato, seeded and chopped

♣ In a medium saucepan combine the water, lentils, onion, and salt. Bring to boiling; reduce heat. Simmer, covered, about 20 minutes or until lentils are tender. Drain off the excess liquid. In a large mixing bowl combine lentil mixture and frozen corn; let stand for 10 minutes.

♣ Meanwhile, in a medium mixing bowl stir together the jicama, sour cream, mayonnaise or salad dressing, and basil. Add the sour cream mixture to the lentil-corn mixture, tossing lightly to coat. Cover and chill for 4 to 24 hours, stirring once or twice.

♣ To serve, stir in the milk to thin the dressing to desired consistency, if necessary. Stir in the tomato. Makes 4 main-dish servings.

Love Those Lentils

Whether lentils really bring wealth and prosperity, as folklore suggests, is open for debate, but one thing is for sure: Lentils are an excellent source of protein. They also supply fiber, calcium, vitamin B, iron, and phosphorus to your diet. With a beanlike texture and a mild, nutty flavor, they're a tasty addition to soups as well as salads, casseroles, and stews.

Layered Vegetable Salad

A sour cream and ranch-style dressing updates this version of a classic. Spread it over the top of the salad before chilling to seal in the freshness of the crisp greens and vegetables.

4 cups torn mixed greens
1 cup small cauliflower flowerets
1 cup halved cherry tomatoes
3 ounces reduced-fat mozzarella cheese, cubed (about ¾ cup)
3 ounces reduced-fat cheddar cheese, cubed (about ¾ cup)
1 cup fresh snow pea pods, tips and strings removed
1 cup shredded carrots
½ cup thinly sliced radishes
¼ cup thinly sliced green onions
⅔ cup light dairy sour cream
¼ cup fat-free ranch salad dressing
1 teaspoon lemon juice
⅛ teaspoon bottled hot pepper sauce

♣ Place mixed greens in a 3-quart salad bowl. Layer atop lettuce in the following order: cauliflower, cherry tomatoes, mozzarella cheese, cheddar cheese, pea pods, carrots, radishes, and green onions.

♣ For dressing, in a small bowl stir together the sour cream, ranch salad dressing, lemon juice, and hot pepper sauce. Spread dressing over top of salad, sealing to edge of bowl. Cover and refrigerate for 2 to 24 hours.

♣ To serve, gently toss to coat vegetables with dressing. Makes 4 main-dish servings.

TOTAL FAT: 10 g
DAILY VALUE FAT: 15%
SATURATED FAT: 6 g
DAILY VALUE SATURATED FAT: 29%

NUTRITION FACTS PER SERVING:

Calories	253
Total Fat	10 g
Saturated Fat	6 g
Cholesterol	32 mg
Sodium	500 mg
Carbohydrate	22 g
Fiber	3 g
Protein	18 g

EXCHANGES:
4 Vegetable
2 Lean Meat
1 Fat

PREPARATION TIME: 20 minutes
CHILLING TIME: 2 hours

Barley-Bean Salad

On a hot summer day, refresh your family with this mint-accented salad for lunch or dinner.
Serve it with crisp crackers, iced tea, and fresh fruit or sherbet for dessert.

2 cups water
1 cup quick-cooking barley
½ of a 15-ounce can reduced-sodium
   garbanzo beans, rinsed and drained
   (¾ cup)
¼ cup shredded carrot
2 tablespoons snipped fresh parsley
1 tablespoon snipped fresh mint or
   1 teaspoon dried mint, crushed
¼ cup lemon juice
1 tablespoon olive oil or salad oil
¼ teaspoon salt
¼ teaspoon pepper
¼ cup cashews or toasted sliced almonds
4 kale leaves or lettuce cups

♣ In a medium saucepan bring the water to boiling. Stir in barley. Return to boiling; reduce heat. Simmer, covered, for 10 to 12 minutes or until barley is tender; drain. Rinse with cold water; drain well.

♣ In a large mixing bowl stir together the drained barley, garbanzo beans, carrot, parsley, and mint.

♣ For dressing, in a screw-top jar combine the lemon juice, oil, salt, and pepper. Cover and shake well. Pour dressing over barley mixture, tossing to coat. Cover and chill for 4 to 24 hours, stirring once or twice.

♣ To serve, stir cashews or almonds into salad. Spoon salad onto kale leaf-lined plates. Makes 4 main-dish servings.

TOTAL FAT: 9
DAILY VALUE FAT: 14%
SATURATED FAT: 1 g
DAILY VALUE SATURATED FAT: 5%

**NUTRITION FACTS
PER SERVING:**

Calories	299
Total Fat	9 g
Saturated Fat	1 g
Cholesterol	0 mg
Sodium	199 mg
Carbohydrate	48 g
Fiber	6 g
Protein	9 g

EXCHANGES:
3 Starch
1 Fat

PREPARATION TIME: 25 minutes
CHILLING TIME: 4 hours

TOTAL FAT: 13 g
DAILY VALUE FAT: 20%
SATURATED FAT: 2 g
DAILY VALUE SATURATED FAT: 10%

**NUTRITION FACTS
PER SERVING:**

Calories	246
Total Fat	13 g
Saturated Fat	2 g
Cholesterol	58 mg
Sodium	282 mg
Carbohydrate	16 g
Fiber	4 g
Protein	20 g

EXCHANGES:
3 Vegetable
2 Lean Meat
1 Fat

PREPARATION TIME: 20 minutes
CHILLING TIME: 2 hours

Caesar-Style Tofu Salad

Besides providing protein, the mild tofu absorbs and helps distribute the flavors of the lemony dressing.

½ teaspoon instant vegetable bouillon
   granules
⅓ cup boiling water
1 egg
2 tablespoons lemon juice
1 tablespoon olive oil
1 small clove garlic, minced
⅛ teaspoon pepper
   Dash Worcestershire sauce
8 cups torn romaine
2 medium carrots, cut into thin strips
1 green onion, thinly sliced
   (2 tablespoons)
6 Melba toast rounds, broken (1 ounce)
¼ cup finely shredded Parmesan cheese
   Freshly ground black pepper
1 10½-ounce package firm or extra-firm
   tofu (fresh bean curd), drained and
   cubed

♣ For dressing, dissolve bouillon granules in boiling water. Let stand 10 minutes or until cooled to room temperature. In a blender container or food processor bowl, combine the bouillon mixture, egg, lemon juice, olive oil, garlic, the ⅛ teaspoon pepper, and the Worcestershire sauce. Cover and blend or process until smooth.

♣ Transfer dressing to a small saucepan. Cook and stir the dressing over low heat for 8 to 10 minutes or until thickened. *Do not boil.* Transfer to a small bowl. Cover surface with plastic wrap and chill for 2 to 24 hours.

♣ To serve, in a large bowl combine the romaine, carrots, green onion, broken Melba toast, and Parmesan cheese. Pour dressing over salad, tossing lightly to coat. Arrange the salad on a large platter. Sprinkle freshly ground pepper over salad. Place tofu cubes atop salad. Makes 4 main-dish servings.

Wild Rice Salad

Nutty wild rice is not really rice at all, but the seed of a marsh grass. It gives this salad a pleasant nutty flavor and chewy texture.

¾ cup wild rice
¾ cup regular brown rice
3 cups water*
2 teaspoons vegetable bouillon granules*
1 10-ounce package frozen baby lima beans
½ teaspoon finely shredded orange peel
½ cup orange juice
⅓ cup vinegar
2 tablespoons soy sauce
1 teaspoon toasted sesame oil
1 teaspoon grated gingerroot
⅛ teaspoon ground black pepper
⅓ cup thinly sliced celery
¼ cup thinly sliced green onions (2)
¼ cup chopped red or green sweet pepper

♣ Rinse the wild rice in strainer under cold running water about 1 minute. In a medium saucepan combine the uncooked wild rice and brown rice, the water, and the bouillon granules.

Bring to boiling; reduce heat. Simmer, covered, for 30 minutes. Add the lima beans; return to boiling. Simmer, covered, about 10 minutes more or until rice is tender and liquid is absorbed. Remove from heat. Cover; let stand for 5 minutes.

♣ Meanwhile, for dressing, in a screw-top jar combine orange peel, orange juice, vinegar, soy sauce, sesame oil, gingerroot, and black pepper. Cover and shake well.

♣ In a large mixing bowl stir together the cooked rice mixture, celery, green onions, and sweet pepper. Pour orange juice mixture over rice mixture, tossing to coat. Cover and chill for 4 to 24 hours, stirring once or twice. Makes 5 main-dish servings.

*Note: You may substitute 3 cups *Vegetable Stock* (see recipe, page 64) for the water and the bouillon granules.

TOTAL FAT: 2 g
DAILY VALUE FAT: 3%
SATURATED FAT: 0 g
DAILY VALUE SATURATED FAT: 0%

**NUTRITION FACTS
PER SERVING:**

Calories	286
Total Fat	2 g
Saturated Fat	0 g
Cholesterol	0 mg
Sodium	809 mg
Carbohydrate	58 g
Fiber	6 g
Protein	11 g

EXCHANGES:
3 Starch
1 Vegetable

PREPARATION TIME: 55 minutes
CHILLING TIME: 4 hours

TOTAL FAT: 9 g
DAILY VALUE FAT: 14%
SATURATED FAT: 2 g
DAILY VALUE SATURATED FAT: 10%

NUTRITION FACTS
PER SERVING:

Calories	385
Total Fat	9 g
Saturated Fat	2 g
Cholesterol	213 mg
Sodium	372 mg
Carbohydrate	65 g
Fiber	3 g
Protein	13 g

EXCHANGES:
4 Starch
1 Medium-Fat Meat

PREPARATION TIME: 20 minutes
BAKING TIME: 55 minutes

Roasted Hot Potato Salad

This robust main dish showcases garlic-roasted vegetables tossed with a warm sweet-sour dressing. It may remind you of hot German potato salad.

Nonstick spray coating
2 pounds whole tiny new potatoes, quartered
1 cup packaged, peeled baby carrots
3 tablespoons lemon juice
1 tablespoon olive oil
1 clove garlic, minced
¼ teaspoon salt
½ cup cold water
2 teaspoons all-purpose flour
2 tablespoons vinegar
2 teaspoons sugar
½ teaspoon celery seed
½ teaspoon dry mustard
¼ teaspoon salt
⅛ teaspoon pepper
1 medium onion, chopped (½ cup)
1 clove garlic, minced
4 hard-cooked eggs
Fresh snipped chives (optional)

♣ Spray a 13×9×2-inch baking pan with nonstick coating. Combine the potatoes and carrots in prepared pan. Spread the vegetables evenly in the pan.

♣ In a small mixing bowl stir together the lemon juice, olive oil, 1 clove garlic, and ¼ teaspoon salt. Drizzle lemon juice mixture over vegetables. Bake, covered, in a 425° oven for 30 minutes. Remove foil, stir vegetables. Bake, uncovered, for 25 to 30 minutes more or until vegetables are tender and starting to brown on edges, stirring occasionally.

♣ In a small mixing bowl stir together the cold water and the flour. Stir in the vinegar, sugar, celery seed, dry mustard, ¼ teaspoon salt, and pepper; set aside.

♣ Spray a large skillet with nonstick coating. Preheat the skillet over medium-high heat. Add the onion and 1 clove garlic; cook until onion is tender. Stir in the flour mixture. Cook and stir until thickened and bubbly. Add the potato-carrot mixture, gently tossing to mix. Cook, stirring gently, for 1 to 2 minutes more or until heated through. Transfer to a serving bowl.

♣ Press 3 of the hard-cooked eggs through a wire sieve. Add sieved eggs to potato mixture, tossing to mix. Slice the remining hard-cooked egg. If desired, arrange slices atop salad; garnish with snipped chives. Makes 4 main-dish servings.

TOTAL FAT: 12 g
DAILY VALUE FAT: 18%
SATURATED FAT: 2 g
DAILY VALUE SATURATED FAT: 10%

**NUTRITION FACTS
PER SERVING:**

Calories	302
Total Fat	12 g
Saturated Fat	2 g
Cholesterol	30 mg
Sodium	288 mg
Carbohydrate	40 g
Fiber	2 g
Protein	12 g

EXCHANGES:

1½ Starch
3 Vegetable
1½ Lean Meat
1½ Fat

START TO FINISH: 20 minutes

Tortellini-Vegetable Salad

A homemade vinaigrette that's short on oil, but long on flavor, gives pasta and greens a low-fat, appealing tang. (Pictured on pages 44 and 45).

1 **9-ounce package refrigerated cheese tortellini**
6 **cups torn mixed greens**
1½ **cups sliced fresh mushrooms**
1 **medium yellow or red sweet pepper, cut into bite-size strips (1 cup)**
¼ **cup snipped fresh basil**
¼ **cup white wine vinegar**
2 **tablespoons water**
2 **tablespoons olive oil**
2 **teaspoons sugar**
2 **cloves garlic, minced**
¼ **teaspoon ground black pepper**
½ **cup fat-free toasted garlic and onion croutons**

♣ In a large saucepan cook the tortellini according to package directions, *except* omit any oil or salt; drain. Rinse with cold water; drain.

♣ In a large mixing bowl combine the cooked tortellini, mixed greens, mushrooms, sweet pepper, and basil.

♣ For dressing, in a screw-top jar combine the white wine vinegar, water, olive oil, sugar, garlic, and black pepper. Cover and shake well. Pour over tortellini mixture, tossing to coat.

♣ To serve, divide the tortellini mixture among 4 serving bowls or plates. Pass the croutons. Makes 4 main-dish servings.

Salad Greens Math

Use this guide to determine how much to buy to make a specified cup measure of greens. Measurements are for loosely packed torn greens:

Butterhead lettuce	1 medium head (12 ounces)	4 cups
Iceberg lettuce	1 medium head (18 ounces)	10 cups
Leaf lettuce	1 medium head (9 ounces)	8 cups
Romaine	1 medium head (16 ounces)	6 cups (ribs removed)
Spinach	16 ounces	12 cups (stems removed)

Bow-Tie & Fruit Salad

In the summer, make this orange-and-honey-sweetened salad with sliced strawberries and chopped nectarines in place of the grapes and apple.

2	**cups packaged dried bow-tie pasta**
1½	**cups seedless green grapes, cut into halves**
1	**cup shredded reduced-fat cheddar or mozzarella cheese (4 ounces)**
1	**medium apple, chopped (about 1 cup)**
1	**stalk celery, thinly sliced (½ cup)**
¾	**cup light dairy sour cream**
1	**teaspoon finely shredded orange peel**
2	**tablespoons orange juice**
1	**tablespoon honey**
¼	**teaspoon ground cardamom or ground cinnamon**
	Orange juice (optional)

♣ In a large saucepan cook bow-tie pasta according to package directions, except omit any oil or salt; drain. Rinse with cold water; drain.

♣ In a large mixing bowl stir together the cooked bow-tie pasta, grapes, cheddar cheese, apple, and celery.

♣ For dressing, in a small mixing bowl stir together the sour cream, orange peel, the 2 tablespoons orange juice, the honey, and cardamom or cinnamon. Spoon dressing over pasta mixture, stirring gently until coated. Cover and chill for 4 to 6 hours. If mixture seems dry after chilling, stir in 1 to 2 tablespoons additional orange juice before serving. Makes 4 main-dish servings.

Salad Savvy: Tips for Great Salads

♣ Clean and chill ingredients ahead of time. Also chill salad plates and bowls.

♣ If a salad includes tomatoes, add them just before tossing to keep them from watering out and diluting the dressing.

♣ Toss a salad with its dressing at the last minute to prevent the dressing from wilting the greens.

♣ Accent salads with simple additions, such as a few olives, toasted nuts, homemade croutons, or broken chow-mein noodles.

TOTAL FAT: 10 g
DAILY VALUE FAT: 15%
SATURATED FAT: 5 g
DAILY VALUE SATURATED FAT: 25%

NUTRITION FACTS
PER SERVING:

Calories	323
Total Fat	10 g
Saturated Fat	5 g
Cholesterol	49 mg
Sodium	275 mg
Carbohydrate	44 g
Fiber	3 g
Protein	15 g

EXCHANGES:
2 Starch
1 Fruit
1 Medium-Fat Meat
½ Fat

PREPARATION TIME: 30 minutes
CHILLING TIME: 4 hours

The New Chef's Salad

What makes a chef's salad a chef's salad? Traditionally, strips of meats and cheeses on top of mixed greens. This meatless version outshines the chef's salads of the '70s with spinach, cabbage, kidney beans, fresh vegetables, and a homemade low-fat dressing.

⅓ cup fat-free mayonnaise dressing or
    salad dressing
⅓ cup light dairy sour cream
2 teaspoons white wine vinegar
2 cloves garlic, minced
1½ teaspoons snipped fresh marjoram or
    ½ teaspoon dried marjoram, crushed
¼ teaspoon dry mustard
⅛ teaspoon salt
3 tablespoons skim milk
2 cups torn Boston or Bibb lettuce
2 cups torn fresh spinach
1 cup shredded red cabbage
1 15-ounce can reduced-sodium kidney
    beans or garbanzo beans, rinsed and
    drained
½ cup halved cherry tomatoes
1 cup shredded low-fat cheddar cheese
    (4 ounces)
1 small zucchini, thinly sliced (about
    1 cup)
1 small green or red sweet pepper, thinly
    sliced (about ¾ cup)
½ cup thinly sliced radishes
1 hard-cooked egg, sliced

♣ In a small mixing bowl combine mayonnaise dressing or salad dressing, sour cream, wine vinegar, garlic, marjoram, mustard, and salt. Stir in the milk.

♣ In a large salad bowl toss together the lettuce, spinach, red cabbage, kidney beans, tomatoes, cheddar cheese, zucchini, sweet pepper, and radishes. Pour the salad dressing over all, tossing to coat. Divide mixture among 4 plates. Arrange egg slices on salad. Makes 4 main-dish servings.

TOTAL FAT: 8 g
DAILY VALUE FAT: 12%
SATURATED FAT: 4 g
DAILY VALUE SATURATED FAT: 20%

NUTRITION FACTS
PER SERVING:

Calories	275
Total Fat	8 g
Saturated Fat	4 g
Cholesterol	76 mg
Sodium	740 mg
Carbohydrate	34 g
Fiber	7 g
Protein	20 g

EXCHANGES:
1 Starch
3 Vegetable
2 Lean Meat

START TO FINISH: 25 minutes

Succotash Soup & Dumplings, recipe on page 75

Tortellini & Vegetable Soup,
recipe on page 65

Satisfying Soups

Nothing warms a hungry crew more than a hearty bowl of soup. Plus, all you need to fill out a soup menu is warm, crusty bread or a small mixed greens salad. From Curried Lentil Stew or Two-Bean Chili to Roasted Garlic Barley Soup or Minestrone, you'll find all the choices tempting.

TOTAL FAT: 2 g
DAILY VALUE FAT: 3%
SATURATED FAT: 0 g
DAILY VALUE SATURATED FAT: 0%

**NUTRITION FACTS
PER CUP:**

Calories	17
Total Fat	2 g
Saturated Fat	0 g
Cholesterol	0 mg
Sodium	313 mg
Carbohydrate	0 g
Fiber	0 g
Protein	0 g

**EXCHANGES:
Free Food**

START TO FINISH: 2 hours 30 minutes

Vegetable Stock

Add robust vegetable flavor to soups, stews, and sauces by starting with your own homemade stock. It's easy to make. Just use a combination of vegetable odds and ends you have on hand or overflows from your garden. You'll need about 15 cups of vegetables total.

> 4 **medium yellow onions**
> 4 **medium carrots**
> 3 **medium potatoes**
> 2 **medium parsnips, turnips, or rutabagas**
> 1 **small head cabbage**
> 1 **tablespoon olive oil**
> 8 **cups water**
> 1 **teaspoon salt**
> ½ **teaspoon dried dillweed or dried basil, rosemary, or marjoram, crushed**
> ¼ **teaspoon pepper**

♣ Scrub all vegetables; remove root and stem ends. Do not peel vegetables, unless coated with wax. Cut onions into wedges. Cut carrots; potatoes; parsnips, turnips, or rutabagas; and cabbage into 2-inch pieces.

♣ Add olive oil to a 6-quart Dutch oven and heat over medium heat. Add vegetables to the Dutch oven. Cook for 10 minutes or until vegetables are starting to brown, stirring frequently. Stir in the water, the salt, desired herb, and pepper. Bring to boiling; reduce heat. Simmer, covered, for 2 hours.

♣ To strain the stock, line a large colander with 2 layers of 100% cotton cheesecloth. Set the colander in a large heatproof bowl or container. Ladle or pour the stock through the lined colander. Discard vegetables and seasonings.

♣ Store stock in a covered container in the refrigerator for up to 3 days or in the freezer for up to 6 months. Makes about 7 cups stock.

Homemade vs. Store-Bought

Although it may not pay to make some things yourself, stock may be worth the effort. If you have an overabundance of vegetables in your garden, making vegetable stock can save your garden from being wasted. Better yet, you don't have to use picture-perfect vegetables either. Homemade stock also saves you about half the sodium of canned stock. So, if you're watching your sodium intake or you have a bountiful garden that's a bit past its prime, making vegetable stock from scratch makes sense. Best of all, *you* control the amount of sodium and the types of vegetables that go into your stock to use in soups and other stock- or broth-based dishes.

Tortellini & Vegetable Soup

Plump tortellini, nutty wild rice, crisp-tender vegetables, and bits of robust dried tomato offer a variety of textures and flavors. (Pictured on pages 62 and 63.)

¼ cup wild rice
  Nonstick spray coating
1 cup chopped onions
½ cup thinly sliced celery
1 clove garlic, minced
6½ cups water*
2 teaspoons instant vegetable bouillon granules*
1 teaspoon dried oregano, crushed
½ teaspoon dried marjoram, crushed
⅛ teaspoon pepper
1 bay leaf
1 9-ounce package refrigerated cheese tortellini
2 cups chopped broccoli flowerets
2 tablespoons snipped dried tomato (not oil-packed)

♣ Rinse wild rice in a strainer under cold running water about 1 minute. Drain; set aside.

♣ Spray a large saucepan with nonstick coating. Preheat over medium-high heat. Add the onions, celery, and garlic. Cook, covered, for 3 to 4 minutes or until vegetables are crisp-tender, stirring once or twice. Carefully stir in wild rice, water, bouillon granules, oregano, marjoram, pepper, and bay leaf. Bring to boiling; reduce heat. Cover and simmer about 35 minutes or until rice is nearly tender. Discard bay leaf.

♣ Add tortellini, broccoli, and dried tomato. Return to boiling; reduce heat. Cook, uncovered, for 5 to 6 minutes more or until tortellini and broccoli are just tender. To serve, ladle soup into bowls. Makes 4 main-dish servings.

*Note: You may substitute 6½ cups *Vegetable Stock* (see recipe, page 64) for the water and the bouillon granules.

TOTAL FAT: 5 g
DAILY VALUE FAT: 8%
SATURATED FAT: 2 g
DAILY VALUE SATURATED FAT: 10%

NUTRITION FACTS
PER SERVING:

Calories	277
Total Fat	5 g
Saturated Fat	2 g
Cholesterol	30 mg
Sodium	746 mg
Carbohydrate	46
Fiber	4 g
Protein	15 g

EXCHANGES:
2 Starch
2 Vegetable
1 Medium-Fat Meat

START TO FINISH: 1 hour

TOTAL FAT: 2 g
DAILY VALUE FAT: 3%
SATURATED FAT: 1 g
DAILY VALUE SATURATED FAT: 5%

NUTRITION FACTS
PER SERVING:

Calories	193
Total Fat	2 g
Saturated Fat	1 g
Cholesterol	2 mg
Sodium	650 mg
Carbohydrate	40 g
Fiber	5 g
Protein	9 g

EXCHANGES:
2 Starch
2 Vegetable

START TO FINISH: 55 minutes

Minestrone

Minestrone means "big soup" in Italian, and this bountiful bean and vegetable stew lives up to its name.

  2 14½-ounce cans vegetable broth or
       3½ cups Vegetable Stock (see recipe,
       page 64)
  1 14½-ounce can low-sodium stewed
       tomatoes, undrained
  1 large potato, coarsely chopped
  1 medium onion, chopped (½ cup)
  1 stalk celery, thinly sliced (½ cup)
  1 carrot, thinly sliced (½ cup)
 1½ teaspoons dried basil, crushed
  1 cup shredded cabbage
  1 15-ounce can great northern beans,
       rinsed and drained
  1 cup frozen whole kernel corn
  ⅓ cup orzo (rosamarina)
  2 tablespoons grated Parmesan cheese

♣ In a large saucepan combine the vegetable broth or stock, the undrained tomatoes, potato, onion, celery, carrot, and basil. Bring to boiling; reduce heat. Simmer, covered, for 10 minutes. Stir in the cabbage, beans, corn, and orzo. Return to boiling; reduce heat. Simmer, covered, for 10 to 15 minutes more or until vegetables and pasta are just tender. To serve, ladle soup into bowls. Top each serving with Parmesan cheese. Makes 6 main-dish servings.

Soup or Stew for Another Day

Soups and stews always make a welcome meal on a cold, wintry day. Leftover soups and stews also make perfect fair-weather meals when you want something nutritious yet fast. To save extra soup or stew, place it in a freezer-safe container. Label the container with the contents or name of the recipe and the date you're freezing it. For the best results and flavor, freeze the soup or stew only up to six months. To serve, transfer the frozen mixture to a large saucepan, cover, and cook over medium-low heat until heated through, stirring occasionally.

TOTAL FAT: 1 g
DAILY VALUE FAT: 2%
SATURATED FAT: 0 g
DAILY VALUE SATURATED FAT: 0%

NUTRITION FACTS
PER SERVING:

Calories	217
Total Fat	1 g
Saturated Fat	0 g
Cholesterol	0 mg
Sodium	495 mg
Carbohydrate	41 g
Fiber	3 g
Protein	13 g

EXCHANGES:
2 Starch
2 Vegetable

PREPARATION TIME: 15 minutes
STANDING TIME: 1 hour
COOKING TIME: 1¾ hours

Herbed Bean Stew

Let your culinary imagination go. Try different combinations of dried beans and your favorite herbs and spices.

1 cup dry navy beans
¾ cup dry red beans
6 cups water
4 cups water*
1 cup chopped onions
2 cloves garlic, minced
2 bay leaves
2 teaspoons instant vegetable bouillon granules*
1 teaspoon sugar
1 teaspoon dried oregano, crushed
½ teaspoon salt
⅛ teaspoon pepper
1½ cups chopped, peeled rutabaga or potato
1 9-ounce package frozen Italian green beans
1 8-ounce can low-sodium tomato sauce

♣ Rinse the navy and red beans. In a 4-quart Dutch oven combine the beans and the 6 cups water. Bring to boiling; reduce heat. Simmer beans for 2 minutes. Remove from heat. Cover and let stand for 1 hour. (Or, soak the beans in water overnight.)

♣ Drain the beans in a colander and rinse, discarding liquid. Return beans to Dutch oven. Add the 4 cups water, the onions, garlic, bay leaves, bouillon granules, sugar, oregano, salt, and pepper. Bring to boiling; reduce heat. Simmer, covered, about 1¼ hours or until beans are tender.

♣ Add rutabaga or potato. Simmer, covered, for 15 minutes. Add green beans. Simmer, covered, for 10 to 15 minutes more or until rutabaga and green beans are tender.

♣ Stir in the tomato sauce; heat through. Discard bay leaf. To serve, ladle soup into bowls. Makes 6 main-dish servings.

*Note: You may substitute 4 cups of *Vegetable Stock* (see recipe, page 64) for the 4 cups water; omit the vegetable bouillon granules.

Creamy Split Pea Soup

Stir a small amount of light dairy sour cream into ordinary pea soup to boost the flavor. Although it tastes rich and flavorful, you won't have to worry a bit with a mere 3 grams of fat per serving.

1¼ cups dry split peas
5 cups water
1 cup chopped onions
1 teaspoon dried marjoram, crushed
½ teaspoon salt
⅛ teaspoon pepper
1 bay leaf
1 cup thinly sliced carrots
1 tablespoon all-purpose flour
½ cup light dairy sour cream
1 cup skim milk

♣ Rinse the split peas. In a large saucepan combine the split peas, water, onions, marjoram, salt, pepper, and bay leaf. Bring to boiling; reduce heat. Simmer, covered, for 1 hour. Stir in carrots. Return to boiling; reduce heat. Simmer, covered, about 20 minutes more or until split peas and carrots are tender. Discard bay leaf.

♣ In a small bowl stir flour into sour cream. Stir sour cream mixture and milk into split pea mixture. Cook and stir until thickened and bubbly. Cook and stir for 1 minute more. Ladle soup into bowls. Serve immediately. Makes 4 main-dish servings.

Healthful Eating Tips

♣ Include more dark green, leafy vegetables in your diet by adding greens such as spinach and kale to sandwiches, salads, vegetable side dishes, and stir-fries.

♣ Add shredded cabbage, especially high-fiber red cabbage, to salads, stir-fries, sandwich fillings, and soups.

♣ Stock up on deep yellow and dark green fruits and vegetables, which are a rich source of vitamin A. These include apricots, cantaloupe, peaches, carrots, sweet potatoes, winter squashes, spinach, broccoli, and Swiss chard.

♣ Boost your fiber intake by cooking with a variety of grains such as couscous, barley, brown rice, oatmeal, rye, wild rice, and bulgur.

TOTAL FAT: 3 g
DAILY VALUE FAT: 5%
SATURATED FAT: 1 g
DAILY VALUE SATURATED FAT: 5%

NUTRITION FACTS PER SERVING:

Calories	307
Total Fat	3 g
Saturated Fat	1 g
Cholesterol	5 mg
Sodium	374 mg
Carbohydrate	52 g
Fiber	4 g
Protein	20 g

EXCHANGES:
2½ Starch
1 Vegetable
1 Lean Meat
½ Milk

PREPARATION TIME: 20 minutes
COOKING TIME: 1 hour 20 minutes

TOTAL FAT: **2 g**
DAILY VALUE FAT: **3%**
SATURATED FAT: **0 g**
DAILY VALUE SATURATED FAT: **0%**

NUTRITION FACTS
PER SERVING:

Calories	210
Total Fat	2 g
Saturated Fat	0 g
Cholesterol	0 mg
Sodium	940 mg
Carbohydrate	44 g
Fiber	9 g
Protein	12 g

EXCHANGES:
2 Starch
3 Vegetable

PREPARATION TIME: **15 minutes**
COOKING TIME: **1 hour 15 minutes**

Wheat Berry-Vegetable Soup

Wheat berries add an intriguing chewy texture, as well as protein and fiber, to this home-style bean and vegetable soup. Look for them in health food stores or with the ready-to-cook cereals in your supermarket.

2 14½-ounce cans vegetable broth or
     3½ cups Vegetable Stock (see recipe,
     page 64)
1 cup water
¼ cup wheat berries
1 15-ounce can great northern beans,
     rinsed and drained
1 14½-ounce can low-sodium tomatoes,
     cut up, undrained
2 cups loose-pack frozen zucchini, carrots,
     cauliflower, lima beans, and Italian
     beans
1 cup chopped onions
3 tablespoons snipped fresh parsley
1 teaspoon dried Italian seasoning,
     crushed
2 cloves garlic, minced
     Grated Parmesan cheese (optional)

♣ In a large saucepan combine the vegetable broth, water, and wheat berries. Bring to boiling; reduce heat. Simmer, covered, 45 to 60 minutes or until wheat berries are tender.

♣ Add the great northern beans, undrained tomatoes, frozen vegetables, onions, parsley, Italian seasoning, and garlic to the saucepan. Bring mixture to boiling; reduce heat. Simmer, covered, for 15 to 20 minutes or until the vegetables are tender.

♣ To serve, ladle soup into bowls. If desired, sprinkle each serving with Parmesan cheese. Makes 4 main-dish servings.

Packing Protein

The average healthy woman needs about 45 grams of protein a day. A healthy man needs about 55 grams. Vegetarians can get protein from several sources:
   ♣ Dairy: milk, yogurt, cheese
   ♣ Eggs
   ♣ Grains and cereals: wheat (bread, flour, pasta), barley, millet, corn, rice, oats, rye
   ♣ Legumes: peas, beans, peanuts, lentils
   ♣ Nuts: walnuts, almonds, pine nuts, hazelnuts, pecans
   ♣ Seeds: sesame seeds, pumpkin seeds, sunflower kernels
   ♣ Soy products: tofu, tempeh, veggie burgers, soy milk, soy cheese, soy ice cream

Two-Bean Chili

Hominy is dried white or yellow corn kernels which have a portion of the kernel removed. It has a soft, chewy texture with a smoky-sour flavor. If you like, substitute 2 cups whole kernel corn for the hominy in this meatless chili.

1 tablespoon olive oil or cooking oil
1 cup chopped onion
½ cup chopped green sweet pepper
2 cloves garlic, minced
1 15¼-ounce can reduced-sodium kidney beans, rinsed and drained
1 15-ounce can pinto beans, rinsed and drained
1 15-ounce can hominy, drained
1¾ cups Vegetable Stock (see recipe, page 64) or one 14½-ounce can vegetable broth
1 14½-ounce can low-sodium stewed tomatoes, undrained
1 4½-ounce can diced green chili peppers, drained
2 teaspoons chili powder
1 teaspoon dried basil, crushed

♣ In a 4-quart Dutch oven heat oil over medium-high heat. Add onion, sweet pepper, and garlic. Cook until vegetables are tender, stirring occasionally. Stir in kidney beans, pinto beans, hominy, stock or broth, *undrained* stewed tomatoes, green chili peppers, chili powder, and basil. Bring to boiling; reduce heat. Simmer, covered, for 20 minutes. To serve, ladle soup into bowls. Makes 5 main-dish servings.

TOTAL FAT: 4 g
DAILY VALUE FAT: 6%
SATURATED FAT: 1 g
DAILY VALUE SATURATED FAT: 5%

NUTRITION FACTS PER SERVING:

Calories	235
Total Fat	4 g
Saturated Fat	1 g
Cholesterol	0 mg
Sodium	776 mg
Carbohydrate	44 g
Fiber	10 g
Protein	11 g

EXCHANGES:
2 Starch
2 Vegetable
½ Fat

START TO FINISH: 45 minutes

Curried Lentil Stew

High in protein and fiber, lentils give an enticing earthy vegetable flavor to all types of soups and stews. Look for lentils near the dried beans in your supermarket.

½ cup chopped onion
1½ to 2 teaspoons curry powder
2 teaspoons cooking oil
2½ cups water
2 cups cubed rutabagas or turnips
1 cup sliced carrots
1 cup dry lentils, rinsed and drained
¼ teaspoon salt
⅛ teaspoon pepper
1 9-ounce package frozen cut green beans
3 cups vegetable juice

♣ In a large saucepan cook onion and curry powder in hot oil for 3 minutes, stirring occasionally. Add water, rutabagas, carrots, lentils, salt, and pepper. Bring to boiling; reduce heat. Simmer, covered, for 15 to 20 minutes or until vegetables and lentils are almost tender.

♣ Stir the frozen green beans into the lentil mixture. Return to boiling; reduce heat. Simmer, covered, for 6 to 8 minutes more or until vegetables and lentils are tender. Stir in the vegetable juice and heat through. To serve, ladle into soup bowls. Makes 6 main-dish servings.

Fiber for Thought

Fiber often gets put on a pedestal when it comes to healthful food choices—and with good reason. A high-fiber diet may help lower the risk of heart disease and some cancers. The health bonuses of fiber may be due to other components found in high-fiber foods, not from the fiber alone. That is why it is best to reap the benefits of fiber from foods rather than supplements. Fiber is found only in plant foods such as whole-grain breads and cereals, beans, legumes, fruits, and vegetables. Because various foods contain different types of fiber, it is best to choose a variety of fiber-rich foods daily.

TOTAL FAT: 2 g
DAILY VALUE FAT: 3%
SATURATED FAT: 0 g
DAILY VALUE SATURATED FAT: 0%

NUTRITION FACTS PER SERVING:

Calories	106
Total Fat	2 g
Saturated Fat	0 g
Cholesterol	0 mg
Sodium	566 mg
Carbohydrate	24 g
Fiber	4 g
Protein	5 g

EXCHANGES:
1 Starch
2 Vegetable

START TO FINISH: 45 minutes

TOTAL FAT: 2 g
DAILY VALUE FAT: 3%
SATURATED FAT: 0 g
DAILY VALUE SATURATED FAT: 0%

NUTRITION FACTS
PER SERVING:

Calories	173
Total Fat	2 g
Saturated Fat	0 g
Cholesterol	0 mg
Sodium	642 mg
Carbohydrate	35 g
Fiber	7 g
Protein	6 g

EXCHANGES:
1½ Starch
2 Vegetable

PREPARATION TIME: 5 minutes
BAKING TIME (Garlic): 25 minutes
COOKING TIME: 20 minutes

Roasted Garlic Barley Soup

Roasting garlic sweetens and mellows its characteristically strong flavor. So, don't be timid about using the entire head.

1	medium head garlic
1	teaspoon olive oil or cooking oil
4	cups water*
1½	cups thinly sliced leeks
¾	cup thinly sliced celery
2	teaspoons instant vegetable bouillon granules*
1½	teaspoons dried basil, crushed
⅛	teaspoon pepper
1	14½-ounce can tomatoes, undrained and cut up
1	medium zucchini or yellow summer squash, halved lengthwise and thinly sliced
½	cup quick-cooking barley

♣ Peel away the outer dry leaves from the head of garlic, leaving skin of garlic cloves intact. Cut off pointed top portion of head (about ¼ inch) with a knife, leaving the bulb intact but exposing the individual cloves. Place garlic head, cut side up, in a small baking dish; drizzle with the oil. Bake garlic, covered, in a 400° oven for 25 to 35 minutes or until cloves feel soft when pressed. Cool slightly. Press garlic pulp from individual cloves; mash pulp with a fork.

♣ In a large saucepan combine the garlic paste, water, leeks, celery, bouillon granules, basil, and pepper. Bring to boiling; reduce heat. Simmer, covered, about 10 minutes or until leeks and celery are tender. Stir in the undrained tomatoes, zucchini or squash, and barley. Return soup to boiling; reduce heat. Simmer, covered, about 10 minutes more or until the barley is tender. To serve, ladle the soup into bowls. Makes 4 main-dish servings.

*Note: You may substitute 4 cups of *Vegetable Stock* (see recipe, page 64) for the water and the bouillon granules.

Succotash Soup & Dumplings

To cut fresh corn from the cob, hold each ear of corn so an end rests on a cutting board. Then, with a sharp knife, cut down the ear from top to bottom, cutting through the base of each kernel. (Pictured on page 62.)

3 cups water*
2 cups cut fresh corn or one 10-ounce package frozen whole kernel corn
1 cup frozen lima beans
½ cup chopped celery
½ cup sliced carrot
½ cup chopped onion
2 teaspoons instant vegetable bouillon granules*
1 tablespoon snipped fresh dill or ½ teaspoon dried dillweed
1 cup water
⅓ cup yellow cornmeal
¼ teaspoon salt
   Dash pepper
1 beaten egg
⅔ cup all-purpose flour
1 tablespoon grated Parmesan cheese
1 tablespoon snipped fresh parsley
1 teaspoon baking powder
⅓ cup packaged instant mashed potato flakes

♣ In a large saucepan combine the 3 cups water, corn, lima beans, celery, carrot, onion, bouillon granules, and dill. Bring to boiling; reduce heat. Simmer, covered, for 8 to 10 minutes or until vegetables are almost tender.

♣ Meanwhile, for dumplings, in a medium saucepan combine the 1 cup water, cornmeal, salt, and pepper. Cook and stir until thickened and bubbly. Remove from heat; cool slightly. Add the egg, beating until smooth. Stir together the flour, Parmesan cheese, parsley, and baking powder. Add to the cornmeal mixture; beat well. Set aside.

♣ Stir the instant mashed potato flakes into the soup. Cook and stir until slightly thickened and bubbly. Drop dumpling mixture from a tablespoon into 8 mounds directly on top of the bubbling soup. Cover and simmer for 10 to 12 minutes (*do not lift cover*) or until a toothpick inserted in a dumpling comes out clean. To serve, ladle soup and dumplings into bowls. Makes 4 main-dish servings.

*Note: You may substitute 3 cups of *Vegetable Stock* (see recipe, page 64) for the 3 cups water and the bouillon granules.

TOTAL FAT: 3 g
DAILY VALUE FAT: 5%
SATURATED FAT: 1 g
DAILY VALUE SATURATED FAT: 5%

NUTRITION FACTS
PER SERVING:

Calories	279
Total Fat	3 g
Saturated Fat	1 g
Cholesterol	55 mg
Sodium	765 mg
Carbohydrate	55 g
Fiber	4 g
Protein	11 g

EXCHANGES:
3 Starch
1 Vegetable

START TO FINISH: 45 minutes

Cheesy Vegetable Chowder

Gruyère cheese is known for its rich, sweet, nutty flavor. We recommend aged Gruyère, which usually is produced in France. Processed Gruyère just can't compare in the flavor of the aged variety.

2 cups water*
2 cups cubed potatoes
¾ cup chopped onion
½ cup chopped celery
1 tablespoon snipped fresh thyme or
    ½ teaspoon dried thyme, crushed
2 teaspoons instant vegetable bouillon
    granules*
⅛ teaspoon ground black pepper
2 cups cut fresh corn or frozen whole
    kernel corn
2 cups chopped cabbage
¼ cup chopped green sweet pepper
2 cups skim milk
2 tablespoons all-purpose flour
1 cup shredded Gruyère or Swiss cheese
    (4 ounces)
Fresh thyme leaves (optional)

♣ In a large saucepan combine the water, potato, onion, celery, the 1 tablespoon fresh thyme, bouillon granules, and black pepper. Bring to boiling; reduce heat. Simmer, covered, for 10 minutes. Stir in the corn, cabbage, and sweet pepper. Cook, covered, about 5 minutes more or until the potatoes and corn are just tender, stirring occasionally.

♣ Meanwhile, in a screw-top jar shake together *½ cup* of the milk and the flour. Stir milk-flour mixture and remaining milk into potato mixture in saucepan. Cook and stir until thickened and bubbly. Cook and stir for 1 minute more. Remove from heat. Add the Gruyère or Swiss cheese, stirring until melted. To serve, ladle soup into bowls. If desired, garnish with additional fresh thyme. Makes 5 main-dish servings.

*Note: You may substitute 2 cups of *Vegetable Stock* (see recipe, page 64) for the 2 cups water and the bouillon granules.

TOTAL FAT: 9 g
DAILY VALUE FAT: 14%
SATURATED FAT: 5 g
DAILY VALUE SATURATED FAT: 25%

**NUTRITION FACTS
PER SERVING:**

Calories	288
Total Fat	9 g
Saturated Fat	5 g
Cholesterol	26 mg
Sodium	512 mg
Carbohydrate	41 g
Fiber	6 g
Protein	15 g

EXCHANGES:
2 Starch
1 Vegetable
1 Medium-Fat Meat
½ Milk

START TO FINISH: 40 minutes

TOTAL FAT: 5 g

DAILY VALUE FAT: 8%

SATURATED FAT: 3 g

DAILY VALUE SATURATED FAT: 15%

NUTRITION FACTS
PER SERVING:

Calories	180
Total Fat	5 g
Saturated Fat	3 g
Cholesterol	15 mg
Sodium	658 mg
Carbohydrate	22 g
Fiber	2 g
Protein	12 g

EXCHANGES:

2 Vegetable

1 Medium-Fat Meat

½ Milk

START TO FINISH: 30 minutes

Beer & Cheese Soup

Thought you gave up splurge foods, such as cheese soup? Reduced-fat cheese means you can have your cheese soup and eat it, guilt-free, too. Add a bit of crunch by floating a toast triangle or a few herb-seasoned croutons on each serving.

2	cups sliced fresh mushrooms
1½	cups chopped carrots
1	cup water
¾	cup chopped red or green sweet pepper
¾	cup chopped onion
2½	cups skim milk
⅓	cup all-purpose flour
¼	teaspoon ground white pepper
½	cup beer
8	ounces light processed cheese product, cubed, or 2 cups shredded reduced-fat sharp cheddar cheese (8 ounces)

♣ In a large saucepan combine the mushrooms, carrots, water, sweet pepper, and onion. Bring to boiling; reduce heat. Simmer, covered, for 3 to 4 minutes or until vegetables are just tender. *Do not drain.*

♣ Meanwhile, in a screw-top jar shake together *1 cup* of the milk and the flour. Add milk-flour mixture to vegetables in saucepan along with the remaining milk and white pepper. Cook and stir until thickened and bubbly. Cook and stir for 1 minute more. Stir in the beer; heat through. Reduce heat. Stir in cheese until melted. Makes 6 main-dish servings.

Cooking With Reduced-Fat Cheeses

Reduced-fat cheeses take a little extra care when cooked. Follow these Better Homes and Gardens ® Test Kitchen tips to get the best results:

♣ Watch carefully when broiling or toasting cheese-topped dishes. The direct heat from a broiler or toaster oven tends to toughen reduced-fat cheeses. Remove the food from the oven just as the cheese begins to melt.

♣ Shred or cube reduced-fat cheeses, just as you do regular cheese, before adding them to sauces and soups. This will help them melt more easily. With the heat on low, add cheese at the end of the cooking time, stirring slowly, just until melted.

♣ Add cheeses gradually to sauces and soups. A large amount added all at once cools the mixture down, which causes cheese to take longer to melt and toughens it.

♣ Prevent cheese soups or sauces from boiling. Boiling causes the cheese to toughen.

Hot-&-Sour Tofu Soup

The smooth-textured cubes of tofu contrast well with the crisp-tender vegetables, and absorb the piquant flavors of rice wine vinegar, soy sauce, and gingerroot.

5 cups water*
¼ cup rice wine vinegar or white vinegar
2 tablespoons reduced-sodium soy sauce
2 teaspoons instant vegetable bouillon
  granules*
1½ teaspoons grated gingerroot
1 teaspoon sugar
¼ to ½ teaspoon pepper
2 cups thinly sliced fresh mushrooms
4 medium green onions, cut into ½-inch
  pieces (½ cup)
1 10½-ounce package light tofu (fresh
  bean curd), cubed
¾ cup bite-size strips of bamboo shoots
½ cup chopped water chestnuts
2 tablespoons cold water
2 tablespoons cornstarch
2 beaten eggs

♣ In a 4-quart Dutch oven combine the 5 cups water, vinegar, soy sauce, bouillon granules, gingerroot, sugar, and pepper. Bring to boiling; reduce heat. Simmer, covered, for 2 minutes. Add mushrooms and green onions. Return to boiling; reduce heat. Simmer, covered, for 2 minutes more. Add tofu, bamboo shoots, and water chestnuts. Return to boiling.

♣ Meanwhile, in a small bowl stir together the 2 tablespoons cold water and cornstarch. Stir cornstarch mixture into tofu mixture in Dutch oven. Cook and stir until slightly thickened and bubbly. Cook and stir for 2 minutes more. Pour the eggs into the soup in a steady stream while stirring 2 or 3 times to create shreds. Serve immediately. Makes 5 main-dish servings.

*Note: You may substitute 5 cups of *Vegetable Stock* (see recipe, page 64) for the water and the bouillon granules.

TOTAL FAT: 3 g
DAILY VALUE FAT: 5%
SATURATED FAT: 0 g
DAILY VALUE SATURATED FAT: 0%

**NUTRITION FACTS
PER SERVING:**

Calories	99
Total Fat	3 g
Saturated Fat	0 g
Cholesterol	86 mg
Sodium	643 mg
Carbohydrate	10 g
Fiber	1 g
Protein	8 g

EXCHANGES:
2 Vegetable
1 Lean Meat

START TO FINISH: 35 minutes

Nutty Orzo and Vegetables, recipe on page 82

Ravioli With Fresh Tomato Sauce,
recipe on page 83

Just Pasta

Pasta comes in so many sizes, shapes, and flavors that the many ways to make it are endless. Cheese Ravioli With Fresh Tomato Sauce and Nutty Orzo and Vegetables are just two of the inviting pasta dishes you'll want to prepare. Portobello Mushroom Stroganoff, Lasagna With Zucchini and Walnuts, and Pasta With Jalapeño-Cheese Sauce are other must-try recipes.

TOTAL FAT: **7 g**
DAILY VALUE FAT: **11%**
SATURATED FAT: **2 g**
DAILY VALUE SATURATED FAT: **10%**

NUTRITION FACTS
PER SERVING:

Calories	313
Total Fat	7 g
Saturated Fat	2 g
Cholesterol	4 mg
Sodium	364 mg
Carbohydrate	53 g
Fiber	7 g
Protein	13 g

EXCHANGES:
2½ Starch
3 Vegetable
½ Fat

START TO FINISH: **15 minutes**

Nutty Orzo & Vegetables

Check the pasta aisle carefully—tiny, rice-shaped orzo may be labeled rosamarina. (Pictured on page 80.)

½ cup packaged dried orzo (rosamarina)
2 cups loose-pack frozen mixed vegetables
1 15-ounce can garbanzo beans, rinsed and drained
1 14½-ounce can low-sodium stewed tomatoes, undrained
1¼ cups purchased light spaghetti sauce
1 tablespoon fresh snipped thyme
¼ cup chopped cashews or slivered almonds, toasted
¼ cup shredded reduced-fat mozzarella cheese (1 ounce)
   Fresh thyme (optional)

♣ In a large saucepan cook the orzo according to package directions, *except* omit salt. Add vegetables after 5 minutes. Drain orzo and vegetables; return to pan. Add garbanzo beans, *undrained* tomatoes, spaghetti sauce, and snipped thyme. Bring to boiling; reduce heat. Simmer, covered, for 5 minutes.

♣ Before serving, stir in cashews or almonds. Divide pasta mixture among 4 dinner plates or bowls. Sprinkle each serving with mozzarella cheese. If desired, garnish with fresh thyme. Makes 4 main-dish servings.

Folic Acid Facts

Folic acid, or folate, is a B vitamin that plays an important role in reducing the risk of a serious type of spinal birth defect in newborns. It is important for child-bearing women to eat enough folic acid before they even become pregnant. A vegetarian diet is abundant in folic acid. Some good sources of folic acid include:

♣ Dry beans (red beans, navy beans, soybeans), lentils, chickpeas, cow peas, peanuts

♣ Fruits (blackberries, boysenberries, kiwifruit, oranges, plantains, strawberries, orange juice, pineapple juice)

♣ Vegetables, including leafy greens (spinach, cabbage, brussels sprouts, romaine, looseleaf lettuce), peas, okra, beets, broccoli, sweet corn

Ravioli With Fresh
Tomato Sauce

To retain the optimum flavor of fresh herbs, add herbs at the end of long periods of cooking rather than in the beginning. Dried herbs, however, can be added in the beginning. (Pictured on pages 80 and 81.)

Nonstick spray coating
1 teaspoon olive oil or cooking oil
1 medium onion, cut into thin wedges
¼ cup thinly sliced celery
¼ cup chopped green sweet pepper
2 cloves garlic, minced
3 cups chopped, peeled tomatoes (3 large)
¼ cup dry red wine or vegetable broth
2 teaspoons sugar
¼ teaspoon salt
⅛ teaspoon ground black pepper
2 tablespoons snipped fresh basil or
    1 teaspoon dried basil, crushed
1 tablespoon snipped fresh oregano or
    ½ teaspoon dried oregano, crushed
1 9-ounce package refrigerated light
    cheese ravioli
Fresh oregano (optional)
Cooked baby patty pan squash, halved
    (optional)

♣ For sauce, spray a large saucepan with nonstick coating; add the 1 teaspoon oil. Preheat over medium-high heat. Add the onion, celery, sweet pepper, and garlic. Cook for 3 to 4 minutes or until the vegetables are tender, stirring occasionally.

♣ Carefully stir in the tomatoes, wine or broth, sugar, salt, black pepper, and, if using, the dried basil and oregano. Bring to boiling; reduce heat. Simmer, uncovered, for 30 to 35 minutes or to desired consistency, stirring occasionally. Stir in the fresh snipped basil and oregano, if using. Cook for 5 minutes more.

♣ Meanwhile, cook ravioli according to package directions, *except* omit any oil or salt. Drain well. Serve the sauce over the hot cooked ravioli. If desired, garnish with fresh oregano and patty pan squash. Makes 3 main-dish servings.

TOTAL FAT: 10 g
DAILY VALUE FAT: 15%
SATURATED FAT: 4 g
DAILY VALUE SATURATED FAT: 20%

**NUTRITION FACTS
PER SERVING:**

Calories	382
Total Fat	10 g
Saturated Fat	4 g
Cholesterol	35 mg
Sodium	661 mg
Carbohydrate	57 g
Fiber	3 g
Protein	19 g

EXCHANGES:
2½ Starch
3 Vegetable
1 Medium-Fat Meat
½ Fat

START TO FINISH: 55 minutes

Spicy Pasta Primavera

Light sour cream and just a sprinkling of Parmesan cheese give the taste and flavor of richness without excessive fat and calories.

8   ounces packaged dried spaghetti
1   cup water
1   teaspoon instant vegetable bouillon
      granules
2   teaspoons snipped fresh tarragon or
      ¼ teaspoon dried tarragon, crushed
¼   teaspoon crushed red pepper
2   cups fresh or frozen Brussels sprouts,
      halved*
1½ cups fresh or frozen cut green beans
1   cup peeled, diced potatoes
1   cup thinly sliced carrots
4   green onions, cut into bite-size pieces
2   tablespoons dry white wine, vegetable
      broth, or water
1   8-ounce carton light dairy sour cream
2   tablespoons all-purpose flour
2   tablespoons grated Parmesan cheese
      Crushed red pepper (optional)

♣ Cook spaghetti according to package directions, *except* omit any oil or salt. Drain and keep warm.

♣ Meanwhile, in a large saucepan combine the water, bouillon granules, tarragon, and the ¼ teaspoon crushed red pepper. Bring to boiling. Add the Brussels sprouts, green beans, potatoes, carrots, and onions. Return to boiling; reduce heat. Simmer, covered, for 10 to 12 minutes or until vegetables are crisp-tender.

♣ Stir wine, broth, or water into the vegetable mixture. In a small mixing bowl stir together the sour cream and flour. Add sour cream mixture to saucepan. Cook and stir until thickened and bubbly. Cook and stir for 1 minute more. Stir in the Parmesan cheese. Serve the sauce over the cooked spaghetti. If desired, sprinkle additional crushed red pepper over each serving. Makes 4 main-dish servings.

*Note: Partially thaw the frozen Brussels sprouts to halve.

TOTAL FAT: 6 g
DAILY VALUE FAT: 9%
SATURATED FAT: 3 g
DAILY VALUE SATURATED FAT: 15%

NUTRITION FACTS
PER SERVING:

Calories	429
Total Fat	6 g
Saturated Fat	3 g
Cholesterol	10 mg
Sodium	385 mg
Carbohydrate	78 g
Fiber	7 g
Protein	17 g

EXCHANGES:
4 Starch
3 Vegetable
½ Fat

START TO FINISH: 45 minutes

TOTAL FAT: 3 g
DAILY VALUE FAT: 5%
SATURATED FAT: 1 g
DAILY VALUE SATURATED FAT: 5%

NUTRITION FACTS
PER SERVING:

Calories	408
Total Fat	3 g
Saturated Fat	1 g
Cholesterol	6 mg
Sodium	281 mg
Carbohydrate	75 g
Fiber	6 g
Protein	21 g

EXCHANGES:
4½ Starch
1 Vegetable
½ Milk

START TO FINISH: 30 minutes

Pasta With Jalapeño-
Cheese Sauce

The ridges in the corkscrew (rotini) pasta trap the bold flavors of the spirited jalapeño pepper and cheddar cheese sauce.

8 ounces packaged dried rotini
1 cup sliced cauliflower flowerets
1 cup sliced fresh mushrooms
¼ cup sliced green onions (2)
¾ cup evaporated skim milk
3 tablespoons all-purpose flour
¾ cup beer
1 15-ounce can reduced-sodium dark red kidney beans, rinsed and drained
1 tablespoon bottled chopped green jalapeño peppers
¼ cup shredded reduced-fat cheddar or mozzarella cheese (1 ounce)

♣ Cook rotini according to package directions, *except* omit any oil or salt. Drain and keep warm.

♣ Meanwhile, in a medium saucepan cook the cauliflower, mushrooms, and green onions in a small amount of *boiling water* for 3 to 4 minutes or until the vegetables are crisp-tender. Drain and set aside.

♣ In a covered screw-top jar shake together the evaporated milk and flour until combined. Add to the saucepan. Stir in beer. Cook and stir over medium heat until thickened and bubbly. Cook and stir for 1 minute more. Stir in the vegetable mixture, kidney beans, and jalapeño peppers. Heat through; reduce heat. Add cheddar or mozzarella cheese; stir until cheese is melted. Serve cheese mixture over the cooked rotini. Makes 4 main-dish servings.

Bean Wisdom

If you're a sodium-watcher, replacing canned beans with cooked beans in recipes can save you considerable amounts of sodium. For example, ½ cup of cooked navy beans (no salt added) contains 1 mg sodium. The same amount of canned navy beans contains more than 580 mg.

A 15-ounce can of beans equals about 1¾ cups drained beans. When a recipe calls for a cup measure of cooked beans, it's helpful to know that 1 pound of dry beans amounts to about 2½ cups uncooked beans and yields about 6 to 7 cups cooked beans.

Pasta With Roasted
Pepper Sauce

For a one-dish meal, add cooked vegetables. Just toss a couple of cups of cut up vegetables, such as asparagus, broccoli, or zucchini, the last few minutes of cooking into the boiling pasta. Drain and toss with the sauce.

2 large red sweet peppers*
8 ounces packaged dried linguine or
    fettuccine
¼ cup chopped onion
¼ cup water
2 teaspoons snipped fresh marjoram or
    ½ teaspoon dried marjoram, crushed
1 teaspoon snipped fresh thyme or
    ¼ teaspoon dried thyme, crushed
⅛ teaspoon salt
½ of an 8-ounce package reduced-fat cream
    cheese (Neufchâtel), cut up
1 cup skim milk
2 tablespoons all-purpose flour
2 tablespoons grated Parmesan cheese

♣ To roast sweet peppers, halve peppers; remove and discard stems, seeds, and membranes. Cut each pepper half in half again. Place peppers, cut sides down, on a foil-lined baking sheet. Press peppers to flatten. Bake in a 425° oven for 20 to 25 minutes or until pepper skins are blistered and dark. Immediately wrap in the foil; let stand about 30 minutes to steam so the skins peel away more easily. Using a paring knife, remove the blistered skin from the peppers, gently and slowly pulling it off in strips. Discard skin.

♣ Cook pasta according to package directions, *except* omit any oil or salt. Drain and return to saucepan; keep warm.

♣ Meanwhile, in a small saucepan combine onion, water, marjoram, thyme, and salt. Bring to boiling; reduce heat. Simmer, covered, for 3 to 4 minutes or until onion is tender. Remove from heat. *Do not drain.* Let stand at room temperature about 5 minutes to cool slightly. Transfer onion mixture to food processor bowl or blender container. Add cream cheese and the roasted peppers. Cover and process or blend until smooth; set aside.

♣ In a medium saucepan, gradually stir milk into flour until smooth; add red pepper mixture. Cook and stir until thickened and bubbly. Cook and stir for 1 minute more. Toss sauce with the cooked pasta. Sprinkle with the Parmesan cheese. Makes 4 main-dish servings.

*Note: If desired, you may substitute ⅔ cup drained, jarred roasted red sweet peppers.

TOTAL FAT: 9 g
DAILY VALUE FAT: 14%
SATURATED FAT: 5 g
DAILY VALUE SATURATED FAT: 25%

NUTRITION FACTS
PER SERVING:

Calories	362
Total Fat	9 g
Saturated Fat	5 g
Cholesterol	25 mg
Sodium	272 mg
Carbohydrate	55 g
Fiber	1 g
Protein	15 g

EXCHANGES:
3½ Starch
1 Vegetable
1 Fat

PREPARATION TIME: 35 minutes
BAKING TIME: 20 minutes
STANDING TIME: 30 minutes

TOTAL FAT: 5 g
DAILY VALUE FAT: 8%
SATURATED FAT: 2 g
DAILY VALUE SATURATED FAT: 10%

NUTRITION FACTS
PER SERVING:

Calories	314
Total Fat	5 g
Saturated Fat	2 g
Cholesterol	11 mg
Sodium	281 mg
Carbohydrate	52 g
Fiber	3 g
Protein	17 g

EXCHANGES:
2 Starch
2 Vegetable
1 Milk

START TO FINISH: 25 minutes

Rotini With Vegetable-
Blue Cheese Sauce

Because of its intense flavor, just a little blue cheese contributes a burst of flavor, yet adds little fat.

6 ounces packaged dried rotini
1 10-ounce package frozen cut asparagus
2 medium carrots, thinly sliced (1 cup)
1 12-ounce can (1½ cups) evaporated
   skim milk
2 tablespoons all-purpose flour
1½ teaspoons snipped fresh marjoram or
   ½ teaspoon dried marjoram, crushed
⅓ cup crumbled blue cheese
   Fresh marjoram (optional)

♣ Cook rotini according to package directions, *except* omit any oil or salt. Drain and keep warm.

♣ Meanwhile, cook the asparagus according to package directions, adding carrots for the last 5 minutes of cooking. Drain and keep warm.

♣ In a medium saucepan whisk together the evaporated milk and flour; add marjoram. Cook and stir over medium heat until thickened and bubbly. Cook and stir for 1 minute more. Stir in the asparagus and carrots. Heat through; remove from heat. Add the blue cheese; stir until cheese is melted. Spoon cheese mixture over cooked rotini. If desired, garnish with fresh marjoram. Makes 3 to 4 main-dish servings.

Cheeses to Please

Depending on your level of vegetarianism, cheese processed in the usual manner may not be an option. Regular cheese typically is made by coagulating milk with animal rennet, which is taken from calves (adult cows do not have this enzyme). "Vegetarian cheeses" are made using rennet derived from fungal or bacterial sources. Be sure to check the label on the cheese you plan to buy. In the future, genetic engineering processes may also produce rennet of nonanimal origin, making regular cheeses a viable option for lacto-ovo vegetarians.

TOTAL FAT: 6 g
DAILY VALUE FAT: 9%
SATURATED FAT: 2 g
DAILY VALUE SATURATED FAT: 10%

NUTRITION FACTS
PER SERVING:

Calories	389
Total Fat	6 g
Saturated Fat	2 g
Cholesterol	6 mg
Sodium	575 mg
Carbohydrate	67 g
Fiber	7 g
Protein	24 g

EXCHANGES:
3½ Starch
2 Vegetable
1 Lean Meat

START TO FINISH: 35 minutes

Fettuccine With
Spinach-Basil Sauce

When you can't find white kidney beans (also called cannellini beans), switch to red kidney beans or black beans; they work equally well.

3 **cups firmly packed, coarsely chopped fresh spinach leaves**
¾ **cup low-fat cottage cheese**
1 **cup firmly packed fresh basil leaves**
⅓ **cup skim milk**
2 **tablespoons grated Parmesan cheese**
2 **cloves garlic, minced**
¼ **teaspoon salt**
8 **ounces packaged dried fettuccine**
1 **15-ounce can white kidney (cannellini) beans, rinsed and drained**
1 **medium zucchini, thinly sliced**
2 **tablespoons pine nuts, toasted**

♣ In a food processor bowl* combine the spinach, cottage cheese, basil leaves, milk, Parmesan cheese, garlic, and salt. Cover and process until nearly smooth, stopping to scrape sides as necessary; set aside.

♣ Cook pasta according to package directions, *except* omit any oil or salt. Add the beans and zucchini for the last 3 minutes of cooking. Drain and return to pan. Quickly add the spinach mixture, tossing to coat pasta with spinach mixture. Cook and stir over low heat until heated through. Sprinkle with pine nuts. Serve immediately. Makes 4 main-dish servings.

***Note:** To use a blender, combine the cottage cheese, milk, Parmesan cheese, garlic, and salt in a blender container. Cover and blend until smooth. Add the spinach and basil, about *one-fourth* at a time, blending until nearly smooth, stopping and pushing greens into blades with a spoon as necessary.

Portobello Mushroom
Stroganoff

Deep brown, giant-size portobello mushrooms have a meaty texture and a rich flavor. Because the stems are very tough, remove and discard them before slicing the caps. If you like, save the stems for long-simmering soups or vegetable stock.

8 ounces packaged dried fettuccine
1 8-ounce carton light dairy sour cream
2 tablespoons all-purpose flour
¾ cup water
1 teaspoon instant vegetable bouillon
   granules
¼ teaspoon pepper
12 ounces portobello mushrooms
   Nonstick spray coating
1 tablespoon margarine or butter
2 medium onions, cut into thin wedges
1 clove garlic, minced
   Snipped fresh parsley

♣ Cook fettuccine according to package directions, *except* omit any oil or salt. Drain and keep warm.

♣ In a small mixing bowl stir together the sour cream and flour. Stir in the water, bouillon granules, and pepper. Set aside.

♣ Remove stems from mushrooms; quarter and thinly slice mushroom tops and set aside.

♣ Spray an unheated large skillet with nonstick coating. Add the margarine or butter and heat over medium-high heat until melted. Add the mushrooms, onions, and garlic. Cook and stir until the vegetables are tender. Stir the sour cream mixture into the skillet. Cook and stir until thickened and bubbly. Cook and stir for 1 minute more. Pour the mushroom mixture over the hot cooked fettuccine, tossing gently to coat. Sprinkle with the snipped parsley. Makes 4 main-dish servings.

TOTAL FAT: 8 g
DAILY VALUE FAT: 12%
SATURATED FAT: 3 g
DAILY VALUE SATURATED FAT: 15%

NUTRITION FACTS
PER SERVING:

Calories	376
Total Fat	8 g
Saturated Fat	3 g
Cholesterol	0 mg
Sodium	320 mg
Carbohydrate	63 g
Fiber	2 g
Protein	14 g

EXCHANGES:
3 Starch
3 Vegetable
1 Fat

START TO FINISH: 25 minutes

Lemony Alfredo-Style
Fettuccine

Have you sworn off pasta Alfredo because it's so high in fat? With this luscious Alfredo-like sauce, you can indulge any time you like. Reduced-fat cream cheese and evaporated skim milk help keep the fat in check.

2   cups loose-pack frozen mixed vegetables
8   ounces packaged dried spinach
    fettuccine or plain fettuccine
2   ounces reduced-fat cream cheese
    (Neufchâtel), cut up
½   cup evaporated skim milk
¼   cup grated Parmesan cheese
½   teaspoon finely shredded lemon peel
¼   teaspoon freshly ground black pepper
    Dash ground nutmeg

♣ Cook the mixed vegetables according to package directions, *except* omit any salt. Drain and keep warm.

♣ Cook the fettuccine according to package directions until tender but still firm, *except* omit any oil or salt. Drain; return the fettuccine to the warm pan.

♣ Add cooked vegetables, cream cheese, evaporated milk, Parmesan cheese, lemon peel, pepper, and nutmeg to saucepan. Heat through, tossing gently until cream cheese is melted and fettuccine is well coated. Serve immediately. Makes 4 main-dish servings.

TOTAL FAT: 6 g
DAILY VALUE FAT: 9%
SATURATED FAT: 4 g
DAILY VALUE SATURATED FAT: 20%

NUTRITION FACTS
PER SERVING:

Calories	339
Total Fat	6 g
Saturated Fat	4 g
Cholesterol	17 mg
Sodium	256 mg
Carbohydrate	55 g
Fiber	1 g
Protein	16 g

EXCHANGES:
3 Starch
1 Vegetable
½ Milk
½ Fat

START TO FINISH: 25 minutes

TOTAL FAT: 5 g
DAILY VALUE FAT: 8%
SATURATED FAT: 1 g
DAILY VALUE SATURATED FAT: 5%

NUTRITION FACTS
PER SERVING:

Calories	254
Total Fat	5 g
Saturated Fat	1 g
Cholesterol	3 mg
Sodium	278 mg
Carbohydrate	45 g
Fiber	5 g
Protein	12 g

EXCHANGES:
2½ Starch
2 Vegetable
½ Fat

START TO FINISH: 30 minutes

Pasta With Beans

Handy, time-saving Italian seasoning usually includes oregano, basil, and rosemary as well as a little ground red pepper and garlic powder all in one neat package.

8 ounces tri-colored rotini
1 tablespoon olive oil
1 medium onion, thinly sliced (¾ cup)
1 medium zucchini or yellow summer
   squash, thinly sliced (1⅓ cups)
2 cloves garlic, minced
1 tablespoon dried Italian seasoning,
   crushed
½ teaspoon sugar
¼ teaspoon salt
¼ teaspoon pepper
1 14½-ounce can low-sodium tomatoes,
   undrained and cut up
1 15-ounce can white kidney (cannellini)
   beans or one 15-ounce can great
   northern beans, rinsed and drained
2 cups shredded fresh spinach
¼ cup finely shredded Parmesan cheese
   (1 ounce)

♣ Cook rotini according to package directions until tender but still firm, *except* omit any oil or salt. Drain and keep warm.

♣ Meanwhile, add the oil to a large saucepan; tilt pan to coat bottom with oil. Add onion, zucchini or squash, garlic, Italian seasoning, sugar, salt, and pepper. Cook over medium-high heat until vegetables are just tender. Carefully add the *undrained* tomatoes and beans. Cover and cook over medium heat for 5 minutes. Stir in the spinach; heat through. Toss with the cooked pasta. Sprinkle with Parmesan cheese. Makes 6 main-dish servings.

Keeping Pasta Warm

What do you do when the pasta is done, but the sauce has a few more minutes to cook? To keep the pasta warm without overcooking it, drain the pasta in a metal colander. Then place the colander over a slightly smaller pot of boiling water (partially cover the colander with a lid). The steam from the water keeps the pasta warm and prevents it from drying out.

Ricotta-&-Feta-Stuffed Shells

Team these ricotta-and-feta cheese-stuffed shells with steamed broccoli spears and a loaf of Italian bread, and your dinner worries are over.

12 packaged dried jumbo shell pasta
2 egg whites
1½ cups low-fat ricotta cheese
½ cup crumbled feta cheese with basil and tomato (2 ounces)
⅛ teaspoon pepper
1 14½-ounce can low-sodium stewed tomatoes, undrained
½ of a 6-ounce can low-sodium tomato paste (⅓ cup)
1 tablespoon snipped fresh basil or 1 teaspoon dried basil, crushed
2 teaspoons snipped fresh oregano or ½ teaspoon dried oregano, crushed
½ teaspoon garlic powder
½ teaspoon sugar
¼ cup finely shredded Parmesan cheese (1 ounce)

♣ Cook jumbo shell pasta according to package directions, *except* omit any oil or salt. Drain; rinse with cold water. Drain again. Place shells, upside down, on a sheet of foil. Set aside.

♣ In a large mixing bowl beat the egg whites with a fork. Stir in the ricotta cheese, feta cheese, and pepper. Spoon about *2 tablespoons* of the cheese mixture into each shell. Arrange the filled shells in a 2-quart square baking dish; set aside.

♣ For the sauce, in a medium saucepan stir together the *undrained* stewed tomatoes, tomato paste, basil, oregano, garlic powder, and sugar. Bring to boiling; reduce heat. Simmer, covered, for 5 minutes. Spoon the sauce over the shells in the baking dish.

♣ Bake shells, covered, in a 375° oven for 20 to 25 minutes or until heated through. To serve, sprinkle the Parmesan cheese over the shells. Makes 4 main-dish servings.

TOTAL FAT: 12 g
DAILY VALUE FAT: 18%
SATURATED FAT: 5 g
DAILY VALUE SATURATED FAT: 25%

**NUTRITION FACTS
PER SERVING:**

Calories	334
Total Fat	12 g
Saturated Fat	5 g
Cholesterol	49 mg
Sodium	581 mg
Carbohydrate	33 g
Fiber	3 g
Protein	23 g

EXCHANGES:
2 Starch
1 Vegetable
2 Medium-Fat Meat

PREPARATION TIME: 30 minutes
BAKING TIME: 20 minutes

TOTAL FAT: 5 g
DAILY VALUE FAT: 8%
SATURATED FAT: 1 g
DAILY VALUE SATURATED FAT: 5%

NUTRITION FACTS
PER SERVING:

Calories	261
Total Fat	5 g
Saturated Fat	1 g
Cholesterol	5 mg
Sodium	562 mg
Carbohydrate	47 g
Fiber	7 g
Protein	13 g

EXCHANGES:
2½ Starch
2 Vegetable
½ Fat

START TO FINISH: 30 minutes

Mexican-Style Pasta

This will surely be a favorite with the kids. If you'd like to add a festive touch of color, use a yellow pepper instead of a green one, or add ½ cup of frozen corn kernels with the tomatoes.

2   teaspoons olive oil or cooking oil
1   cup chopped onions
½   cup chopped green sweet pepper
1½ to 2 teaspoons chili powder
1   14½-ounce can low-sodium tomatoes, undrained and cut-up
1   8-ounce can tomato sauce
½   teaspoon garlic powder
⅛   teaspoon ground red pepper
1   cup wagon wheel pasta or elbow macaroni
1   15½-ounce can reduced-sodium kidney beans, rinsed and drained
¼   cup shredded reduced-fat cheddar cheese (1 ounce)

♣ In a medium saucepan heat the oil over medium-high heat. Add the onions and sweet pepper; cook and stir about 3 minutes or until vegetables are tender. Stir in the chili powder; cook and stir 1 minute. Stir in the *undrained* tomatoes, tomato sauce, garlic powder, and ground red pepper. Bring to boiling; reduce heat. Simmer, uncovered, about 15 minutes or until desired consistency, stirring often.

♣ Meanwhile, cook wagon wheel pasta or elbow macaroni according to package directions, *except* omit any oil or salt; drain. Stir kidney beans and hot cooked pasta into tomato mixture; heat through. Sprinkle with shredded cheddar cheese. Makes 4 main-dish servings.

Compare Your Fat Intake

The fat intake of a nonvegetarian diet ("average diet") compared to various levels of a vegetarian diet differs greatly. As you can see, lacto-vegetarian and vegan diets generally fall below the recommended diet of 30% calories from fat and 10% or less calories from saturated fat (both of these are considered *maximum* percentages). Note the higher range of fat for lacto-vegetarians. To keep it in the lower range, choose low-fat dairy products:

	% Calories From Fat	% Calories From Saturated Fat
Recommended diet	30	<10
Average diet	37	13
Lacto-vegetarian	18 to 48	7
Vegan	15	2

TOTAL FAT: 6 g
DAILY VALUE FAT: 9%
SATURATED FAT: 4 g
DAILY VALUE SATURATED FAT: 20%

NUTRITION FACTS
PER SERVING:

Calories	266
Total Fat	6 g
Saturated Fat	4 g
Cholesterol	27 mg
Sodium	269 mg
Carbohydrate	28 g
Fiber	0 g
Protein	26 g

EXCHANGES:
1 Starch
1 Vegetable
2 Lean Meat
½ Milk

PREPARATION TIME: 30 minutes
BAKING TIME: 30 minutes

Lasagna With
Swiss Cheese Sauce

To dry the spinach thoroughly, drain it in a colander, then wrap it in a kitchen towel, twisting the ends in opposite directions to squeeze out remaining water.

8 packaged dried lasagna noodles
2 egg whites
1 15-ounce carton low-fat or fat-free ricotta cheese
1 10-ounce package frozen chopped spinach, thawed and well drained
6 ounces reduced-fat Swiss cheese, finely chopped
½ cup grated Parmesan cheese
¼ teaspoon ground nutmeg (optional)
Nonstick spray coating
1½ cups sliced fresh mushrooms
½ cup thinly sliced green onions (4)
1 12-ounce can (1½ cups) evaporated skim milk
2 tablespoons all-purpose flour
¼ teaspoon salt (optional)
Paprika

♣ Cook lasagna noodles according to package directions, *except* omit any oil or salt. Drain; rinse with cold water. Drain again. Place noodles, in a single layer, on a sheet of foil; set aside.

♣ For filling, in a large mixing bowl beat the egg whites with a fork. Stir in the ricotta cheese, spinach, *half* of the Swiss cheese, the Parmesan cheese, and, if desired, the nutmeg.

♣ Spray a 2-quart rectangular baking dish with nonstick coating. Spread about ⅓ cup of the filling on each lasagna noodle. Starting from an end, roll up each noodle. Place the lasagna rolls, seam sides down, in the prepared baking dish; set aside.

♣ For sauce, spray an unheated medium saucepan with nonstick coating. Preheat over medium-high heat. Add mushrooms and green onions; cook and stir about 3 minutes or until vegetables are tender. In a medium mixing bowl stir together ¼ *cup* of the evaporated milk and the flour until smooth; stir in the remaining evaporated milk and, if desired, the salt. Stir the flour mixture into the mushroom mixture in the saucepan. Cook and stir until thickened and bubbly. Remove from heat. Stir in the remaining Swiss cheese until melted. Pour the sauce over the lasagna rolls in the baking dish.

♣ Bake rolls, covered, in a 350° oven for 25 to 30 minutes or until lasagna rolls are heated through. To serve, sprinkle with paprika. Makes 8 main-dish servings.

Lasagna With Zucchini
& Walnuts

Toasting the walnuts intensifies their flavor. For ease, "toast" them in your microwave oven. Place them in a small microwave-safe container and microwave on 100% power (high) for 1 to 2 minutes, stirring about every 30 seconds, until toasted and fragrant.

2 **large carrots, finely chopped**
2 **large onions, finely chopped**
2 **medium zucchini, thinly sliced**
2 **cups purchased light spaghetti sauce**
1 **tablespoon snipped fresh basil or**
  1 **teaspoon dried basil, crushed**
2 **cloves garlic, minced**
⅛ **teaspoon pepper**
1 **cup shredded reduced-fat mozzarella cheese (4 ounces)**
¼ **cup grated Parmesan cheese**
  Nonstick spray coating
6 **no-boil lasagna noodles***
¼ **cup finely chopped walnuts, toasted**

♣ For sauce, in a covered medium saucepan cook carrots and onions in a small amount of *boiling water* for 5 minutes. Add zucchini and cook, covered, for 3 to 5 minutes more or until vegetables are tender. Drain thoroughly; return to saucepan. Stir in spaghetti sauce, basil, garlic,

and pepper. Bring to boiling; reduce heat. Simmer, covered, for 10 minutes, stirring occasionally. In a small bowl toss together the mozzarella cheese and Parmesan cheese; set aside.

♣ Spray a 2-quart square baking dish with nonstick coating. Place *two* noodles in bottom of dish. Spread with *one-third* of the sauce mixture. Sprinkle with *one-third* of the walnuts. Sprinkle with *one-third* of the cheese mixture. Repeat layers twice more, *except* end with walnuts; set aside remaining cheese mixture.

♣ Bake lasagna, covered, in a 375° oven for 20 minutes. Uncover and sprinkle with the remaining cheese mixture. Bake, uncovered, about 20 minutes more or until lasagna is heated through. Let stand for 15 minutes before serving. Makes 6 main-dish servings.

*****Note:** Not all brands of no-boil lasagna noodles are the same size. Use enough to have three even, single layers.

TOTAL FAT: 8 g
DAILY VALUE FAT: 12%
SATURATED FAT: 1 g
DAILY VALUE SATURATED FAT: 5%

**NUTRITION FACTS
PER SERVING:**

Calories	229
Total Fat	8 g
Saturated Fat	1 g
Cholesterol	10 mg
Sodium	226 mg
Carbohydrate	30 g
Fiber	4 g
Protein	12 g

EXCHANGES:
1 Starch
3 Vegetable
1 Medium-Fat Meat

PREPARATION TIME: 30 minutes
BAKING TIME: 40 minutes
STANDING TIME: 15 minutes

Lo Mein With Tofu

Look for soba noodles, a type of Japanese pasta made from buckwheat flour, at Asian specialty markets or in the oriental food section of your supermarket.

2   cups broccoli flowerets
1   cup thinly sliced carrots
4   ounces extra-firm light tofu (fresh bean
    curd), cut into ½-inch cubes
1   cup cold water
2   tablespoons reduced-sodium soy sauce
4   teaspoons cornstarch
½   teaspoon instant vegetable bouillon
    granules
8   ounces soba noodles (buckwheat
    noodles) or packaged dried spaghetti
    Nonstick spray coating
1   teaspoon toasted sesame oil
1   cup thinly sliced fresh mushrooms
4   large green onions, cut into ½-inch-long
    pieces
2   teaspoons grated gingerroot
2   cloves garlic, minced
1   tablespoon olive oil or cooking oil
2   teaspoons toasted sesame seeds

♣ In a covered medium saucepan cook the broccoli and carrots in a small amount of *boiling water* for 3 to 4 minutes or until crisp-tender; drain. Set vegetables aside. Pat the tofu dry with paper towels. In a small mixing bowl stir together the cold water, soy sauce, cornstarch, and bouillon granules; set aside.

♣ Cook noodles according to package directions until tender but still firm, *except* omit any oil or salt. Drain and keep warm.

♣ Spray an unheated nonstick wok or large skillet with nonstick coating. Add ½ *teaspoon* of the sesame oil; heat over medium-high heat. Add the mushrooms, green onions, gingerroot, and garlic. Stir-fry for 1 to 2 minutes or until vegetables are crisp-tender. Remove vegetables. Add the olive oil or cooking oil and remaining sesame oil to the wok. Add the tofu; stir-fry for 1 to 2 minutes or just until tofu starts to brown. Remove the tofu. Add the broccoli-carrot mixture and mushroom mixture to the wok; push vegetables from center of the wok. Stir the soy sauce mixture; add to center of wok. Cook and stir until thickened and bubbly.

♣ Add the noodles to the wok or skillet. Using 2 spatulas or forks, lightly toss the mixture for 3 to 4 minutes or until the noodles are heated through. Add the tofu; toss lightly. Cover and cook 1 to 2 minutes or until heated through. To serve, sprinkle with toasted sesame seeds. Makes 4 main-dish servings.

TOTAL FAT: 5 g
DAILY VALUE FAT: 8%
SATURATED FAT: 1 g
DAILY VALUE SATURATED FAT: 5%

NUTRITION FACTS
PER SERVING:

Calories	241
Total Fat	5 g
Saturated Fat	1 g
Cholesterol	0 mg
Sodium	704 mg
Carbohydrate	43 g
Fiber	3 g
Protein	10 g

EXCHANGES:
2 Starch
2 Vegetable
1 Fat

START TO FINISH: 25 minutes

Split Pea Tacos, recipe page 109

Hoppin' John With Grits Polenta, recipe page 104

Beans, Grains, & Legumes

The health benefits of beans, whole grains, and legumes are many. Include them in meals when you can. Hoppin' John With Grits Polenta, Spicy Bean Pizza, or Barley-Stuffed Peppers are all stellar examples.

TOTAL FAT: 4 g
DAILY VALUE FAT: 6%
SATURATED FAT: 1 g
DAILY VALUE SATURATED FAT: 5%

NUTRITION FACTS
PER SERVING:

Calories	295
Total Fat	4 g
Saturated Fat	1 g
Cholesterol	6 mg
Sodium	244 mg
Carbohydrate	54 g
Fiber	5 g
Protein	12 g

EXCHANGES:
3 Starch
2 Vegetable

Polenta:
PREPARATION TIME: 5 minutes
CHILLING TIME: Overnight
COOKING TIME: 9 minutes

Hoppin' John:
START TO FINISH: 35 minutes

Hoppin' John With
Grits Polenta

According to tradition, eating hoppin' John on New Year's Day brings good luck. This appealing version has an Italian slant. (Pictured on pages 102 and 103.)

¾ cup long grain rice
½ of a 16-ounce package frozen black-eyed
    peas or one 15-ounce can black-eyed
    peas, rinsed and drained
1½ cups chopped red, yellow, and/or green
    sweet peppers
1 cup thinly bias-sliced carrots (2 medium)
1 cup frozen whole kernel corn
1 tablespoon finely chopped shallots or
    onion
4 cloves garlic, minced
2 teaspoons freshly snipped thyme or
    1 teaspoon dried thyme, crushed
¼ teaspoon salt
¼ teaspoon red pepper flakes
⅛ teaspoon ground black pepper
2 teaspoons olive oil or cooking oil
2 medium tomatoes, seeded and chopped
2 tablespoons snipped fresh parsley
1 recipe Grits Polenta
    Fresh thyme (optional)

♣ Cook the rice according to package directions, *except* omit any salt. If using frozen black-eyed peas, cook peas according to the package directions; drain.

♣ In a 12-inch skillet cook sweet peppers, carrots, corn, shallots or onion, garlic, thyme, salt, red pepper flakes, and black pepper in hot oil, covered, for 6 to 8 minutes or until vegetables are crisp-tender, stirring occasionally.

♣ Add the cooked rice, black-eyed peas, and tomatoes to the skillet. Stir gently to combine. Cook, covered, over low heat about 5 minutes or until heated through, stirring occasionally. Stir in the snipped fresh parsley. Serve with Grits Polenta. If desired, garnish with fresh thyme. Makes 6 main-dish servings.

Grits Polenta: In a medium saucepan combine 1⅓ cups *water,* ⅔ cup *skim milk,* and ⅛ teaspoon *salt.* Bring to boiling; reduce heat. Add ½ cup *quick-cooking white (hominy) grits,* stirring with a whisk. Cook and stir for 5 to 7 minutes or until very thick. Remove from heat. Add ½ cup shredded *reduced-fat mozzarella cheese,* stirring until melted. Spray a 9-inch pie plate with *nonstick coating.* Spread grits mixture into the pie plate. Cover and chill overnight. Cut firm grits into 12 wedges. Spray the rack of an unheated broiler pan with nonstick spray coating. Arrange wedges on the prepared pan. Broil 4 to 5 inches from heat for 4 to 5 minutes or until the surface is slightly crisp and beginning to brown.

Spicy Bean Pizza

No ordinary pizza, this all-vegetable pie combines a lower-fat cornmeal crust with a Mexican-style homemade sauce. If you like, substitute a refrigerated pizza crust for the homemade cornmeal pizza crust.

1 cup chopped onion
3 cloves garlic, minced
2 teaspoons olive oil or cooking oil
1 14½-ounce can low-sodium tomatoes, undrained and cut up
1 8-ounce can low-sodium tomato sauce
1½ cups chopped zucchini
¾ cup chopped green sweet pepper
1½ teaspoons chili powder
½ teaspoon sugar
½ teaspoon dried oregano, crushed
¼ teaspoon salt
⅛ to ¼ teaspoon ground red pepper
1 recipe Cornmeal Pizza Crust
 Nonstick spray coating
1 15¼-ounce can reduced-sodium dark red kidney beans, rinsed and drained
1 15½-ounce can reduced-sodium garbanzo beans, rinsed and drained
1 cup shredded reduced-fat mozzarella cheese (4 ounces)

♣ In a large saucepan cook and stir the onion and garlic in hot oil over medium-high heat about 3 to 4 minutes or until the onion is tender. Stir in the *undrained* tomatoes, tomato sauce, zucchini, green pepper, chili powder, sugar, oregano, salt, and ground red pepper. Bring to boiling; reduce heat. Simmer, uncovered, for 35 to 40 minutes or to desired consistency, stirring occasionally.

♣ Meanwhile, prepare Cornmeal Pizza Crust. Cover and let rest for 10 minutes. Spray a 15×10×1-inch baking pan with nonstick coating. On a lightly floured surface, roll dough into a 16×11-inch rectangle. Transfer to pan. Build up edges slightly. If desired, crimp edges. Prick dough generously with a fork. *Do not let rise.* Bake in a 425° oven for 15 to 18 minutes or until lightly browned.

♣ Sprinkle the kidney beans and garbanzo beans over crust. Spoon sauce over beans. Sprinkle with cheese. Bake about 15 minutes more or until heated through. Makes 8 main-dish servings.

Cornmeal Pizza Crust: In a large mixing bowl combine 1½ cups *all-purpose flour*, 1 package *active dry yeast*, and ¼ teaspoon *salt*. Add 1 cup *warm water* (120° to 130°) and 2 tablespoons *olive oil* or *cooking oil*. Beat with an electric mixer on low speed for 30 seconds, scraping bowl constantly. Beat on high speed for 3 minutes. Using a spoon, stir in ¾ cup *yellow cornmeal* and as much of ½ to 1 cup *all-purpose flour* as you can. Turn dough out onto a lightly floured surface. Knead in enough of the remaining flour to make a moderately stiff dough that is smooth and elastic (6 to 8 minutes total).

TOTAL FAT: 8 g
DAILY VALUE FAT: 12%
SATURATED FAT: 2 g
DAILY VALUE SATURATED FAT: 10%

NUTRITION FACTS
PER SERVING:

Calories	359
Total Fat	8 g
Saturated Fat	2 g
Cholesterol	8 mg
Sodium	388 mg
Carbohydrate	57 g
Fiber	8 g
Protein	16 g

EXCHANGES:
3 Starch
2 Vegetable
1 Lean Meat

PREPARATION TIME: 1 hour
BAKING TIME: 30 minutes

TOTAL FAT: 5 g
DAILY VALUE FAT: 8%
SATURATED FAT: 3 g
DAILY VALUE SATURATED FAT: 15%

NUTRITION FACTS
PER SERVING:

Calories	231
Total Fat	5 g
Saturated Fat	3 g
Cholesterol	65 mg
Sodium	514 mg
Carbohydrate	33 g
Fiber	4 g
Protein	13 g

EXCHANGES:
2 Starch
1 Vegetable
1 Lean Meat

PREPARATION TIME: 20 minutes
BAKING TIME: 22 minutes

Barley-Stuffed Peppers

These stuffed peppers use barley filling instead of Mom's old-fashioned hamburger stuffing, but they're just as comforting. For an eye-catching presentation, use two different colored sweet peppers.

1   cup water
1   cup sliced fresh mushrooms
⅔   cup quick-cooking barley
1   teaspoon instant vegetable bouillon
    granules
2   large red, yellow, and/or green sweet
    peppers (about 1 pound)
1   beaten egg
¾   cup shredded reduced-fat mozzarella
    cheese (3 ounces)
1   large tomato, peeled, seeded, and
    chopped (about ¾ cup)
½   cup shredded zucchini
⅓   cup soft bread crumbs
1   tablespoon snipped fresh basil or
    ½ teaspoon dried basil, crushed
1   teaspoon snipped fresh rosemary or
    ⅛ teaspoon dried rosemary, crushed
¼   teaspoon onion salt
    Several dashes bottled hot pepper sauce
    Fresh rosemary (optional)
    Dried red chili peppers (optional)

♣ In a medium saucepan combine the water, mushrooms, barley, and bouillon granules. Bring to boiling; reduce heat. Simmer, covered, for 12 to 15 minutes or until barley is tender. Drain thoroughly.

♣ Cut sweet peppers in half lengthwise; remove seeds and membranes. If desired, precook pepper halves in *boiling water* for 3 minutes. Drain on paper towels.

♣ In a medium mixing bowl stir together the egg, *½ cup* of the cheese, the tomato, zucchini, bread crumbs, basil, rosemary, onion salt, and bottled hot pepper sauce. Stir in cooked barley mixture. Place peppers, cut side up, in a 2-quart rectangular baking dish. Spoon barley mixture into the pepper halves.

♣ Bake stuffed peppers, covered, in a 350° oven for 20 to 25 minutes or until filling is heated through. Sprinkle remaining cheese over the peppers. Return to oven; bake 2 minutes more. Carefully transfer peppers to a serving platter. If desired, garnish with fresh rosemary and dried red chili peppers. Makes 4 main-dish servings.

TOTAL FAT: 2 g
DAILY VALUE FAT: 3%
SATURATED FAT: 0 g
DAILY VALUE SATURATED FAT: 0%

NUTRITION FACTS
PER SERVING:

Calories	353
Total Fat	2 g
Saturated Fat	0 g
Cholesterol	0 mg
Sodium	465 mg
Carbohydrate	70 g
Fiber	7 g
Protein	15 g

EXCHANGES:

4 Starch
1 Vegetable

PREPARATION TIME: 20 minutes
SOAKING TIME: 1 hour
COOKING TIME: 1 hour 40 minutes

Savory Beans & Rice

For a mild flavor, use only a drop or two of hot pepper sauce. If you like lots of heat, dash in a little more.

1¼ cups dry red beans or dry red kidney beans
4 cups water
2½ cups water
¾ cup chopped onion
½ cup sliced celery
2 cloves garlic, minced
2 teaspoons instant vegetable bouillon granules
1 teaspoon dried basil, crushed
1 bay leaf
1¼ cups regular brown rice
1 14½-ounce can low-sodium stewed tomatoes, undrained
1 4-ounce can diced green chili peppers, drained
Few dashes bottled hot pepper sauce

♣ Rinse beans. In a large saucepan combine beans and the 4 cups water. Bring to boiling; reduce heat. Simmer for 2 minutes. Remove from heat. Cover and let stand for 1 hour. (Or, place beans in the water in saucepan. Cover and let soak in a cool place for 6 to 8 hours or overnight.) Drain and rinse beans.

♣ Return beans to saucepan. Add the 2½ cups water, the onion, celery, garlic, bouillon granules, basil, and bay leaf. Bring to boiling; reduce heat. Simmer, covered, 1½ to 1¾ hours or until beans are tender, stirring occasionally. Remove bay leaf.

♣ Meanwhile, cook the brown rice according to the package directions, *except* omit the salt. Keep rice warm.

♣ Stir *undrained* stewed tomatoes, chili peppers, and hot pepper sauce into cooked beans. Bring to boiling; reduce heat. Simmer, uncovered, about 10 minutes or to desired consistency. Serve bean mixture over hot cooked brown rice. Makes 5 main-dish servings.

Split Pea Tacos

Take a break from traditional taco fillings and try savory split peas seasoned with onion, garlic, and chili peppers. (Pictured on page 102.)

1 cup dry yellow or green split peas
2½ cups water
1 medium onion, chopped
2 cloves garlic, minced
1 4-ounce can diced green chili peppers, rinsed and drained
1 to 2 teaspoons chili powder
8 taco shells or four 9- to 10-inch flour tortillas
1 cup shredded lettuce
¾ cup chopped tomato
½ cup shredded reduced-fat cheddar or mozzarella cheese (2 ounces)
Salsa or taco sauce (optional)

♣ For filling, rinse the split peas. In a medium saucepan combine the split peas, water, onion, garlic, chili peppers, and chili powder. Bring to boiling; reduce heat. Simmer, covered, about 50 minutes or until split peas are tender.

♣ Meanwhile, heat the taco shells (if using) according to package directions. Spoon filling into shells. Top with lettuce, tomato, and cheese. (Or, if using flour tortillas, wrap in foil. Heat in a 350° oven for 10 minutes to soften. Spoon about ⅔ cup filling onto each tortilla along the center. Top with lettuce, tomato, and cheese. Fold bottom edge of each tortilla up over filling. Fold opposite sides in just to enclose filling. Roll up from the bottom.) If desired, serve with salsa or taco sauce. Makes 4 main-dish servings.

Oh, Sweet Pea

Split peas, also called field peas, are green or yellow round seeds with a mild, sweet flavor and tender texture. Field peas are a legume specifically grown to be dried. They are sold whole as well as split. Look for them next to dry beans in the supermarket.

Because split peas don't have to be soaked before cooking as dry beans do, they are more convenient to use. Split peas cook in about 45 to 50 minutes. One pound of uncooked split peas yields about 5½ cups of cooked peas. One ½-cup serving contains about 8 grams protein, 3 grams fiber, and 115 calories.

TOTAL FAT: 10 g
DAILY VALUE FAT: 15%
SATURATED FAT: 2 g
DAILY VALUE SATURATED FAT: 10%

NUTRITION FACTS
PER SERVING:

Calories	363
Total Fat	10 g
Saturated Fat	2 g
Cholesterol	10 mg
Sodium	299 mg
Carbohydrate	52 g
Fiber	3 g
Protein	19 g

EXCHANGES:
3 Starch
1 Vegetable
1 Medium-Fat Meat
½ Fat

PREPARATION TIME: 10 minutes
COOKING TIME: 50 minutes

Triple Mushroom
& Rice Fajitas

This earthy three-mushroom filling and all the traditional fajita toppers make a satisfying meatless meal. Substitute button mushrooms if you can't find all three varieties of mushrooms in your supermarket.

½ cup regular brown rice
¼ cup water
2 tablespoons lime juice
1 tablespoon olive oil or cooking oil
2 large cloves garlic, minced
½ teaspoon ground cumin
½ teaspoon dried oregano, crushed
¼ teaspoon salt
3 ounces fresh portobello mushrooms, stemmed and thinly sliced
3 ounces fresh chanterelle or oyster mushrooms, thinly sliced
3 ounces fresh shiitake mushrooms, stemmed and thinly sliced
1 medium green and/or red sweet pepper, cut into thin strips
4 green onions, cut into 1½-inch pieces
8 7- to 8-inch flour tortillas
¼ cup slivered almonds, toasted
 Green onion tops (optional)
 Fresh cilantro (optional)

♣ Cook brown rice according to package directions, *except* omit any salt.

♣ Meanwhile, for marinade, in a large plastic bag set in a deep bowl combine the water, lime juice, olive oil or cooking oil, garlic, cumin, oregano, and salt. Add mushrooms, pepper strips, and green onions. Seal the bag; turn bag to coat vegetables. Marinate at room temperature for 15 to 30 minutes.

♣ Wrap tortillas in foil. Heat in a 350° oven for 10 minutes to soften.

♣ For filling, in a large nonstick skillet cook *undrained* mushroom mixture over medium-high heat for 6 to 8 minutes or until peppers are tender and all but about 2 tablespoons of the liquid has evaporated, stirring occasionally. Stir in brown rice and almonds; heat through.

♣ To serve, spoon mushroom-rice mixture onto tortillas; roll up. If desired, tie a green onion top around each tortilla and garnish with cilantro. If desired, serve with *Bibb lettuce, lime wedges,* and *cherry tomatoes.* Makes 4 main-dish servings.

TOTAL FAT: **9 g**
DAILY VALUE FAT: **14%**
SATURATED FAT: **2 g**
DAILY VALUE SATURATED FAT: **10%**

**NUTRITION FACTS
PER SERVING:**

Calories	331
Total Fat	9 g
Saturated Fat	2 g
Cholesterol	0 mg
Sodium	380 mg
Carbohydrate	55 g
Fiber	4 g
Protein	9 g

EXCHANGES:
3 Starch
2 Vegetable
1 Fat

START TO FINISH: 1 hour

TOTAL FAT: 9 g
DAILY VALUE FAT: 14%
SATURATED FAT: 2 g
DAILY VALUE SATURATED FAT: 10%

NUTRITION FACTS
PER SERVING:

Calories	319
Total Fat	9 g
Saturated Fat	2 g
Cholesterol	10 mg
Sodium	478 mg
Carbohydrate	48 g
Fiber	7 g
Protein	17 g

EXCHANGES:
2½ Starch
1 Vegetable
1 Medium-Fat Meat
½ Fat

COOKING TIME: 45 minutes
COOLING TIME (rice): 30 minutes
BAKING TIME: 9 minutes

New Orleans-Style Rice Patties

Reminiscent of Louisiana red beans and rice, these nutty rice patties and their colorful chili-like sauce team up to make a spunky down-home supper.

½ cup regular brown rice
   Nonstick spray coating
2 beaten egg whites or ¼ cup refrigerated
   or frozen egg product, thawed
4 green onions, thinly sliced (½ cup)
¼ cup finely chopped walnuts
¼ cup fine dry bread crumbs
½ teaspoon dried thyme, crushed
¼ teaspoon dried savory or basil, crushed
⅛ teaspoon salt
⅛ teaspoon ground red pepper
¼ cup chopped green sweet pepper
1 15½-ounce can reduced-sodium red
   kidney beans, rinsed and drained
1 8-ounce can low-sodium tomato sauce
½ cup water
1 to 2 teaspoons chili powder
⅛ teaspoon salt
½ cup shredded reduced-fat cheddar cheese
   (2 ounces)

♣ Cook the brown rice according to package directions, *except* omit any salt. Cool the rice for 30 minutes.

♣ Spray a large baking sheet with nonstick coating. In a medium mixing bowl combine the cooled brown rice, the egg whites or egg product, green onions, walnuts, bread crumbs, thyme, savory or basil, the ⅛ teaspoon salt, and the ground red pepper. With wet hands, shape mixture into 8 equal patties, about ½-inch thick. Place patties on the prepared baking sheet. Bake in a 400° oven for 9 to 10 minutes or until patties are heated through.

♣ Meanwhile, spray an unheated medium saucepan with nonstick coating. Preheat over medium-high heat. Add sweet pepper; cook and stir until pepper is tender. Stir in the drained beans, tomato sauce, water, chili powder, and the remaining ⅛ teaspoon salt. Bring to boiling; reduce heat. Simmer, uncovered, for 3 minutes. Mash the beans slightly.

♣ Spoon the bean mixture over the rice patties. Sprinkle with the shredded cheddar cheese. Makes 4 main-dish servings.

Vegetable Fried Rice

To simplify this Asian-inspired brown rice dish, make the rice in advance. Cover and chill it overnight. You'll only need 30 minutes to prepare dinner the next day.

1 tablespoon cooking oil
1 cup finely chopped fresh mushrooms
½ cup thinly sliced green onions
⅓ cup coarsely shredded carrot
⅓ cup thinly sliced fresh pea pods
6 cups cooked brown rice, well chilled
3 tablespoons water
2 tablespoons reduced-sodium soy sauce
2 tablespoons dry sherry (optional)
2 beaten eggs

♣ Add the oil to a 12-inch skillet, tilting skillet to coat; preheat over medium heat just until warm. Add the mushrooms, green onions, carrot, and pea pods. Cook and stir about 2 minutes or until vegetables are just tender. Stir in the chilled rice. Spread mixture evenly in the skillet. Cook over medium heat for 5 minutes without stirring. Stir thoroughly with a metal turner, lifting and turning the browned rice from the bottom of the skillet. Spread rice mixture evenly in skillet; cook for 5 to 7 minutes more or until rice is lightly browned on bottom.

♣ Meanwhile, in a small bowl stir together the water, soy sauce, and sherry, if desired. Stir soy sauce mixture into the rice mixture. Drizzle eggs over; cook for 1 to 2 minutes or until eggs start to set. Stir thoroughly; cook 1 to 2 minutes more or until eggs are set. Makes 4 main-dish servings.

TOTAL FAT: 9 g
DAILY VALUE FAT: 14%
SATURATED FAT: 2 g
DAILY VALUE SATURATED FAT: 10%

NUTRITION FACTS
PER SERVING:

Calories	411
Total Fat	9 g
Saturated Fat	2 g
Cholesterol	107 mg
Sodium	314 mg
Carbohydrate	71 g
Fiber	6 g
Protein	12 g

EXCHANGES:
4½ Starch
1 Vegetable
½ Fat

COOKING/CHILLING TIME (rice):
8 hours
PREPARATION TIME: 15 minutes
COOKING TIME: 15 minutes

Fresh Vegetable Risotto

Be sure to use Italian Arborio rice, with its short, plump grains, for risotto. Constant stirring releases the starch in the rice, giving the risotto its trademark creaminess.

1   tablespoon olive oil or cooking oil
2   cups sliced fresh mushrooms
½   cup chopped onion (1 medium)
2   cloves garlic, minced
1   cup Arborio rice or medium grain rice
3   cups water*
1   teaspoon instant vegetable bouillon
       granules*
2   cups bite-size fresh asparagus pieces or
       fresh broccoli flowerets
¾   cup chopped tomato
¼   cup shredded carrot (1 small)
¾   cup shredded reduced-fat mozzarella
       cheese (3 ounces)
3   tablespoons grated Parmesan cheese
3   tablespoons snipped fresh basil or
       fresh parsley
    Parmesan cheese shavings (optional)
    Fresh basil leaves (optional)

♣ In a large saucepan heat oil over medium heat. Add the mushrooms, onion, and garlic; cook until onion is tender. Stir in the rice. Cook and stir for 5 minutes.

♣ Meanwhile, in another saucepan combine the water and bouillon granules. Bring to boiling; reduce heat. Slowly and carefully add *1 cup* of the broth mixture to the rice mixture, stirring constantly. Continue to cook and stir until liquid is absorbed. Add *½ cup* more broth mixture and the asparagus or broccoli to the rice mixture, stirring constantly. Continue to cook and stir until liquid is absorbed. Add *1 cup* more broth mixture, ½ cup at a time, stirring constantly until the broth mixture has been absorbed. (This should take about 15 minutes.)

♣ Stir in the remaining broth mixture, the tomato, and carrot. Cook and stir until rice is slightly creamy and just tender. Stir in mozzarella cheese, grated Parmesan cheese, and snipped fresh basil. Serve immediately. If desired, garnish each serving with Parmesan shavings and fresh basil leaves. Makes 4 main-dish servings.

*__Note:__ You may substitute 3 cups *Vegetable Stock* (see recipe, page 64) for the water and the bouillon granules.

TOTAL FAT: 8 g
DAILY VALUE FAT: 12%
SATURATED FAT: 2 g
DAILY VALUE SATURATED FAT: 10%

NUTRITION FACTS
PER SERVING:

Calories	320
Total Fat	8 g
Saturated Fat	2 g
Cholesterol	11 mg
Sodium	432 mg
Carbohydrate	49 g
Fiber	3 g
Protein	15 g

EXCHANGES:
2 Starch
3 Vegetable
1 Medium-Fat Meat

START TO FINISH: 40 minutes

TOTAL FAT: 7 g
DAILY VALUE FAT: 11%
SATURATED FAT: 1 g
DAILY VALUE SATURATED FAT: 5%

**NUTRITION FACTS
PER SERVING:**

Calories	312
Total Fat	7 g
Saturated Fat	1 g
Cholesterol	38 mg
Sodium	207 mg
Carbohydrate	53 g
Fiber	4 g
Protein	11 g

EXCHANGES:
2½ Starch
3 Vegetable
1 Fat

PREPARATION TIME: 25 minutes
COOKING TIME (Wheat berries): 45 to 60 minutes

Wheat Berries With Noodles

Vary the flavor of this pasta, vegetable, and grain medley by using different types of mushrooms. Choose traditional milder brown or white mushrooms, or opt for the more exotic chanterelle, shiitake, oyster, crimini, or portobello varieties.

> 6 ounces medium noodles (about 3 cups)
> 1 tablespoon margarine or butter
> 2 medium onions, halved and thinly sliced
> 3 cups sliced fresh mushrooms (8 ounces)
> 2 small zucchini or yellow summer squash, thinly sliced (2 cups)
> ⅓ cup reduced-fat Italian salad dressing or other vinaigrette-type salad dressing
> 1 tablespoon snipped fresh thyme or ½ teaspoon dried thyme, crushed
> ¼ teaspoon coarsely ground pepper
> 1½ cups cooked wheat berries*
> 2 tablespoons snipped fresh parsley

♣ Cook the noodles according to package directions, *except* omit any oil and salt. Drain and keep warm.

♣ In a large saucepan cook and stir the onions, mushrooms, and squash in melted margarine or butter over medium heat for 5 to 7 minutes or until vegetables are tender and liquid is nearly evaporated. Stir in the salad dressing, thyme, and pepper. Cook and stir for 1 minute more.

♣ Stir the cooked wheat berries, hot cooked noodles, and snipped fresh parsley into the mixture in saucepan. Cover and heat through. Makes 4 main-dish servings.

*****Note:** In a medium saucepan bring 2 cups of *water* to boiling. Add ½ cup *wheat berries;* reduce heat. Simmer, covered, for 45 to 60 minutes or until tender; drain. Makes 1½ cups cooked wheat berries.

Mostaccioli With
Herbed Lentil Sauce

Lentils, fragrant basil, and zesty vegetable juice simmer together to make a hearty sauce to spoon over tender tubes of pasta.

¾ cup dry lentils*
2½ cups vegetable juice
1 cup water
1 large onion, thinly sliced and separated into rings
1 stalk celery, thinly sliced (½ cup)
3 tablespoons snipped fresh basil or 1½ teaspoons dried basil, crushed
2 teaspoons sugar
2 bay leaves
¼ teaspoon bottled hot pepper sauce
8 ounces packaged dried mostaccioli or penne
Grated Parmesan cheese (optional)

♣ Rinse lentils. In a large saucepan combine the lentils, vegetable juice, water, onion, celery, basil, sugar, bay leaves, and hot pepper sauce. Bring to boiling; reduce heat. Simmer, covered, about 45 minutes* or until lentils and vegetables are tender. Discard bay leaves.

♣ Meanwhile, cook mostaccioli or penne according to package directions, *except* omit any oil and salt. Drain and keep warm.

♣ To serve, spoon lentil mixture over cooked pasta. If desired, sprinkle with Parmesan cheese. Makes 4 main-dish servings.

*Note: Regular brown lentils (sometimes called "green"), which are the lentils most commonly found in supermarkets, have their outer seed coat intact. Red and yellow lentils have had the seed coat removed and are found in specialty stores such as Middle Eastern or East Indian markets. You can use the red or yellow varieties here; however, they cook faster. Therefore, allow only about 25 minutes cooking time. You also may need to cook the sauce, uncovered, for 5 minutes more to reach the desired consistency.

TOTAL FAT: 2 g
DAILY VALUE FAT: 3%
SATURATED FAT: 0 g
DAILY VALUE SATURATED FAT: 0%

NUTRITION FACTS PER SERVING:

Calories	391
Total Fat	2 g
Saturated Fat	0 g
Cholesterol	0 mg
Sodium	575 mg
Carbohydrate	77 g
Fiber	2 g
Protein	18 g

EXCHANGES:
4 Starch
2 Vegetable

START TO FINISH: 55 minutes

TOTAL FAT: 2 g
DAILY VALUE FAT: 3%
SATURATED FAT: 0 g
DAILY VALUE SATURATED FAT: 0%

**NUTRITION FACTS
PER SERVING:**

Calories	330
Total Fat	2 g
Saturated Fat	0 g
Cholesterol	0 mg
Sodium	320 mg
Carbohydrate	72 g
Fiber	8 g
Protein	9 g

EXCHANGES:
3 Starch
2 Vegetable
1 Fruit

START TO FINISH: 30 minutes

Indian-Style Vegetables
& Rice

You won't even have to eat out to enjoy an Indonesian-inspired meal. In a bit less than 30 minutes, you can have this fragrant vegetable dish ready for dinner at home. (Pictured on front cover.)

¾ **cup uncooked regular brown rice**
   Nonstick spray coating
1 **large red onion, cut into strips**
2 **cloves garlic, minced**
¾ **cup water**
½ **cup apple juice**
2 **medium potatoes, cut into ½-inch**
   chunks
1 **medium carrot, cut into ¼-inch slices**
2 **tablespoons reduced-sodium soy sauce**
2 **to 3 teaspoons curry powder**
1 **teaspoon grated gingerroot**
½ **teaspoon ground cardamom**
¼ **teaspoon ground cinnamon**
2 **cups cauliflower flowerets**
1 **medium zucchini, halved lengthwise and**
   cut into ½-inch slices
1 **cup frozen peas**
⅓ **cup golden raisins**
   Chutney (optional)

♣ Cook the brown rice according to package directions, *except* omit any salt.

♣ Meanwhile, spray an unheated 4½-quart Dutch oven with nonstick coating. Preheat over medium-high heat. Add onion and garlic; cook and stir until onion is tender. Carefully add the water, apple juice, potatoes, carrot, soy sauce, curry powder, gingerroot, cardamom, and cinnamon. Bring to boiling; reduce heat. Simmer, covered, for 10 minutes.

♣ Add the cauliflower, zucchini, peas, and raisins to the Dutch oven. Simmer, covered, for 10 minutes more or until cauliflower is tender. Serve over hot cooked brown rice. If desired, serve with chutney. Makes 4 main-dish servings.

TOTAL FAT: 6 g
DAILY VALUE FAT: 9%
SATURATED FAT: 1 g
DAILY VALUE SATURATED FAT: 5%

**NUTRITION FACTS
PER SERVING:**

Calories	361
Total Fat	6 g
Saturated Fat	1 g
Cholesterol	0 mg
Sodium	585 mg
Carbohydrate	64 g
Fiber	10 g
Protein	16 g

EXCHANGES:
3 Starch
3 Vegetable
½ Fat

START TO FINISH: 25 minutes

Black Bean Burritos

Leave peeling and cutting the avocado until the last minute. The flesh quickly discolors when exposed to air. If necessary, sprinkle the chopped avocado with a little lemon or lime juice to prevent browning.

1   cup finely chopped onion
1   cup sliced fresh mushrooms
½   cup chopped celery
2   15-ounce cans reduced-sodium black
     beans, rinsed and drained
1   16-ounce can low-sodium tomatoes,
     undrained and cut up
1   ¼-inch-thick slice lemon
1   to 2 fresh jalapeño peppers, seeded and
     finely chopped*
1   tablespoon chili powder
2   cloves garlic, minced
1   teaspoon ground cumin
1   teaspoon dried oregano, crushed
     Dash bottled hot pepper sauce (optional)
8   7- to 8-inch flour tortillas
½   cup salsa
½   of a small avocado, peeled and chopped
     (optional)
¼   cup chopped tomato

♣ In a large saucepan cook onion, mushrooms, and celery in a small amount of *boiling water* until tender. Drain.

♣ Return vegetables to saucepan. Stir in black beans, *undrained* tomatoes, lemon slice, jalapeño peppers, chili powder, garlic, cumin, oregano, and hot pepper sauce, if desired. Bring to boiling; reduce heat. Simmer, uncovered, about 15 minutes or until thick.

♣ Remove lemon slice. In a blender container or food processor bowl place *one-fourth* of the bean mixture (about 1 cup). Cover and blend or process until smooth. Return blended mixture to the bean mixture in the saucepan; heat through.

♣ Meanwhile, wrap tortillas in foil. Heat in a 350° oven for 10 minutes to soften. Divide bean mixture among tortillas, spooning onto tortillas just below the center. Fold in 2 adjacent sides of the tortillas just until they meet; roll up. Serve with salsa, avocado (if desired), and chopped tomato. Makes 4 main-dish servings.

*Note: Protect your hands when working with hot peppers by wearing plastic or rubber gloves or working with plastic bags on your hands. If your bare hands touch the peppers, wash your hands and under your nails thoroughly with soap and water. Avoid rubbing your mouth, nose, eyes, or ears when working with hot peppers.

Italian-Style Shepherd's Pie

Long ago, cooks created Shepherd's Pie to use up leftover mashed potatoes and roast from Sunday's dinner. This modern vegetarian adaptation uses lima and navy beans for protein in place of meat.

2　medium potatoes
2　cloves garlic, minced
½　teaspoon dried basil, crushed
2　teaspoons margarine or butter
⅛　teaspoon salt
2　to 4 tablespoons skim milk
1　10-ounce package frozen lima beans or
　　cut green beans
1　medium onion, chopped (½ cup)
1　medium carrot, thinly sliced (½ cup)
1　15-ounce can navy beans, rinsed and
　　drained
1　14½-ounce can low-sodium tomatoes,
　　drained and cut up
1　8-ounce can low-sodium tomato sauce
½　teaspoon sugar
2　teaspoons cornstarch
¾　cup shredded reduced-fat cheddar cheese
　　(3 ounces)

♣ Peel and quarter the potatoes. Cook, covered, in a small amount of *boiling water* for 20 to 25 minutes or until tender; drain.

♣ In a small saucepan cook and stir the garlic and basil in hot margarine or butter for 30 seconds; remove from heat. Mash potatoes with a potato masher or beat with an electric mixer on low speed. Add the garlic mixture to the mashed potatoes along with the salt. Gradually beat in enough of the milk to make fluffy; set aside.

♣ Meanwhile, for the filling, in a medium saucepan cook the frozen beans, onion, and carrot in a small amount of *boiling water* for 5 to 7 minutes or until tender. Drain; return vegetables to saucepan. Stir in navy beans, *drained* tomatoes, tomato sauce, and sugar. Combine cornstarch and 1 tablespoon *water*. Add to the vegetable mixture. Cook and stir until thickened and bubbly.

♣ Transfer the bean mixture to a 2-quart square baking dish. Spoon the mashed potatoes in 4 mounds on top of the bean mixture. Bake in a 375° oven for 20 to 25 minutes or until heated through. Sprinkle with the cheddar cheese; bake for 2 to 3 minutes more or until cheese is melted. Makes 4 main-dish servings.

TOTAL FAT: 7 g
DAILY VALUE FAT: 11%
SATURATED FAT: 3 g
DAILY VALUE SATURATED FAT: 15%

NUTRITION FACTS
PER SERVING:

Calories	400
Total Fat	7 g
Saturated Fat	3 g
Cholesterol	15 mg
Sodium	765 mg
Carbohydrate	64 g
Fiber	7 g
Protein	22 g

EXCHANGES:
3½ Starch
2 Vegetable
1 Medium-Fat Meat

PREPARATION TIME: 35 minutes
BAKING TIME: 22 minutes

Curried Vegetable Stir-Fry

This flavorful vegetable entrée fuses Asian stir-frying with curry and European Brussels sprouts.

2 cups water

1¼ cups quick-cooking pearl barley

1 cup fresh Brussels sprouts or frozen Brussels sprouts, thawed

1 cup cold water

4 teaspoons cornstarch

1 to 2 teaspoons curry powder

1 teaspoon instant vegetable bouillon granules

Nonstick spray coating

2 medium red, yellow, and/or green sweet peppers, cut into bite-size strips (1½ cups)

2 tablespoons thinly sliced green onion

1 cup bias-sliced carrots

¼ cup peanuts

♣ In a medium saucepan bring the 2 cups water to boiling. Slowly add the barley. Return to boiling; reduce heat. Simmer, covered, for 10 to 12 minutes or until barley is tender. If necessary, drain thoroughly.

♣ Meanwhile, cut Brussels sprouts in half. In a saucepan cook Brussels sprouts in a small amount of *boiling water* for 3 minutes. Drain thoroughly; set aside.

♣ For sauce, in a small bowl stir together the 1 cup water, the cornstarch, curry powder, and bouillon granules. Set aside.

♣ Spray an unheated wok or large skillet with nonstick coating. Preheat over medium-high heat. Add sweet peppers and green onion. Stir-fry for 1 minute. Stir in the Brussels sprouts and carrots. Stir-fry for 3 minutes more. Push the vegetables from the center of the wok.

♣ Stir sauce; add to the center of the wok. Cook and stir until thickened and bubbly. Stir to coat all ingredients with sauce. Cook and stir for 2 minutes.* Serve immediately over barley. Sprinkle each serving with some of the peanuts. Make 4 main-dish servings.

***Note:** If desired, add 4 ounces *extra-firm light tofu* (fresh bean curd), cut into ½-inch cubes. Cover and cook about 30 seconds or until heated through.

TOTAL FAT: 6 g
DAILY VALUE FAT: 9%
SATURATED FAT: 1 g
DAILY VALUE SATURATED FAT: 5%

NUTRITION FACTS
PER SERVING:

Calories	320
Total Fat	6 g
Saturated Fat	1 g
Cholesterol	0 mg
Sodium	333 mg
Carbohydrate	59 g
Fiber	8 g
Protein	10 g

EXCHANGES:
3 Starch
2 Vegetable
½ Fat

START TO FINISH: 30 minutes

Grilled Cheese-Veggie Sandwiches, recipe on page 126

Greek Spinach Triangles,
recipe on page 138

Cheese & Eggs

If you enjoy cheese and eggs in your vegetarian menus, these Greek Spinach Triangles with feta cheese will become a favorite. Or, try Southwestern Enchilada Skillet, Broccoli-Ricotta Calzones, or Grilled Cheese-Veggie Sandwiches.

TOTAL FAT: 8 g
DAILY VALUE FAT: 12%
SATURATED FAT: 4 g
DAILY VALUE SATURATED FAT: 20%

NUTRITION FACTS
PER SERVING:

Calories	241
Total Fat	8 g
Saturated Fat	4 g
Cholesterol	20 mg
Sodium	500 mg
Carbohydrate	29 g
Fiber	1 g
Protein	14 g

EXCHANGES:
2 Starch
1 Medium-Fat Meat

PREPARATION TIME: 10 minutes
COOKING TIME: 6 minutes

Grilled Cheese-Veggie
Sandwiches

Who would have thought a grilled cheese sandwich could taste so fresh? Cabbage, tomato, and sweet pepper turn a plain cheese sandwich into a special lunch or light dinner treat. (Pictured on page 124.)

8   slices whole wheat bread
      Nonstick spray coating
4   ounces reduced-fat cheddar cheese
      and/or Swiss cheese, thinly sliced
1   cup finely shredded cabbage
¼   cup chopped green sweet pepper
¼   cup chopped, seeded tomato

♣ Spray 1 side of *two* slices of bread with the nonstick coating. Place bread, sprayed side down, in a large nonstick skillet. Divide *half* of the cheese between the bread slices.

♣ Divide *half* of the cabbage, sweet pepper, and tomato evenly between the two sandwiches. Top each with a slice of cheese. Spray 1 side of *two* more slices of bread with nonstick coating. Place bread on sandwiches, sprayed side up.

♣ Cook sandwiches over medium heat for 3 to 4 minutes or until bread is toasted and cheese is melted, turning once. Keep sandwiches warm while preparing remaining sandwiches. Repeat assembly and cooking with the remaining 2 sandwiches. Makes 4 main-dish servings.

Spray for Success

Nonstick spray coating not only bypasses the mess of greasing pans, but it also saves on fat and calories. For added interest, look for roasted garlic-, olive oil-, and butter-flavored sprays. Compare the difference of using a nonstick spray in place of oil, margarine, or butter:

	Fat (grams)	Calories
Nonstick spray coating (1-second spray)	<1	7
Butter/margarine (1 tablespoon)	12	104
Oil (1 tablespoon)	14	122

Southwestern Enchilada Skillet

When you need a quick-to-fix dinner or lunch, rely on eggs—they're not just for breakfast. Here they get a flavor lift from cheese, picante sauce, and sour cream.

- 3 **6-inch corn tortillas**
- 6 **egg whites***
- 5 **eggs***
- ⅓ **cup skim milk**
- 2 **tablespoons sliced green onion**
- ⅛ **teaspoon garlic powder**
  Nonstick spray coating
- ¼ **cup shredded reduced-fat cheddar cheese
  (1 ounce)**
- ¾ **cup picante sauce**
- 2 **tablespoons sliced pitted ripe olives**
- ¼ **cup fat-free dairy sour cream**

♣ Cut each tortilla into 8 wedges. Spread the wedges on a large baking sheet. Bake tortilla wedges in a 350° oven for 5 to 10 minutes or until dry and crisp; set aside.

♣ Meanwhile, in a medium mixing bowl beat together egg whites, whole eggs, milk, green onion, and garlic powder. Spray an unheated 10-inch skillet with nonstick coating. Preheat skillet over medium heat. Pour egg white mixture into skillet. Cook, without stirring, until mixture begins to set on the bottom and around the edge. Using a spatula or large spoon, lift and fold the partially cooked egg mixture so uncooked portion flows underneath. Continue cooking and folding, over medium heat, for 2 to 3 minutes or until egg mixture is cooked through, but is still glossy and moist.

♣ Sprinkle the shredded cheddar cheese over the eggs. Top each serving with picante sauce, olives, sour cream, and baked tortilla wedges. Make 4 main-dish servings.

***Note:** You may substitute 2 cups *refrigerated or frozen egg product*, thawed, for the egg whites and eggs.

TOTAL FAT: 10 g
DAILY VALUE FAT: 15%
SATURATED FAT: 3 g
DAILY VALUE SATURATED FAT: 15%

**NUTRITION FACTS
PER SERVING:**

Calories	226
Total Fat	10 g
Saturated Fat	3 g
Cholesterol	272 mg
Sodium	608 mg
Carbohydrate	17 g
Fiber	0 g
Protein	18 g

EXCHANGES:
1 Starch
2 Medium-Fat Meat

START TO FINISH: 20 minutes

TOTAL FAT: 10 g
DAILY VALUE FAT: 15%
SATURATED FAT: 2 g
DAILY VALUE SATURATED FAT: 10%

NUTRITION FACTS
PER SERVING:

Calories	306
Total Fat	10 g
Saturated Fat	2 g
Cholesterol	13 mg
Sodium	649 mg
Carbohydrate	40 g
Fiber	2 g
Protein	16 g

EXCHANGES:
2 Starch
2 Vegetable
1 Medium-Fat Meat
½ Fat

PREPARATION TIME: 45 minutes
BAKING TIME: 10 minutes

Veggie Pizza With
Red Pepper Sauce

A roasted pepper sauce pinch hits for traditional tomato sauce in this healthful pizza topped with summer-fresh vegetables. Or, when time is tight, use purchased pizza sauce.

1 **16-ounce Italian bread shell (Boboli)**
1 **recipe Red Pepper Sauce**
1 **medium yellow summer squash or zucchini, thinly sliced (1⅓ cups)**
2 **thinly sliced green onions (¼ cup)**
1 **cup shredded reduced-fat mozzarella cheese (4 ounces)**
1 **medium tomato, thinly sliced**
⅓ **cup fat-free dairy sour cream**
 Finely chopped fresh jalapeño pepper* or snipped fresh cilantro (optional)

♣ Place the bread shell on a 12-inch pizza pan or a large baking sheet. Spread with Red Pepper Sauce. Arrange the squash slices on top. Bake pizza in a 425° oven for 5 minutes. Sprinkle with green onions and mozzarella cheese. Bake for 5 to 7 minutes more or until cheese is melted.

♣ To serve, cut pizza into wedges. Serve with tomato, sour cream, and, if desired, the jalapeño pepper or cilantro. Makes 6 main-dish servings.

Red Pepper Sauce: Line a baking sheet with foil. Halve lengthwise 2 *medium red sweet peppers* and 1 *Anaheim pepper.* *Remove the seeds and membranes. Place peppers, cut sides down, on prepared baking sheet. Bake in a 425° oven for 20 to 25 minutes or until skins are blistered. Wrap in the foil and let stand for 10 minutes to steam. When cool enough to handle, peel off the skins with a paring knife. Coarsely chop peppers.

In a food processor bowl or blender container combine roasted peppers with 1 clove *garlic,* cut up; 1 tablespoon *olive oil;* ¼ teaspoon *salt;* and ¼ teaspoon *ground cumin.* Cover and process or blend until nearly smooth. Makes about ¾ cup.

***Note:** Protect your hands when working with hot peppers by wearing plastic or rubber gloves or working with plastic bags on your hands. If your bare hands touch the peppers, wash your hands and under your nails thoroughly with soap and water. Avoid rubbing your mouth, nose, eyes, or ears when working with hot peppers.

TOTAL FAT: 9 g
DAILY VALUE FAT: 14%
SATURATED FAT: 1 g
DAILY VALUE SATURATED FAT: 5%

NUTRITION FACTS
PER SERVING:

Calories	275
Total Fat	9 g
Saturated Fat	1 g
Cholesterol	6 mg
Sodium	302 mg
Carbohydrate	34 g
Fiber	1 g
Protein	14 g

EXCHANGES:
2 Starch
1 Lean Meat
½ Milk
½ Fat

PREPARATION TIME: 1 hour
BAKING TIME: 40 minutes

Wheat Berry Quiche

Wheat berries, the whole unprocessed kernels of wheat, add a pleasant chewy texture to this vegetable-filled quiche. Look for them in your health food store or with the cooked cereals in your supermarket.

⅓ cup wheat berries
1¼ cups all-purpose flour
½ teaspoon dried basil, crushed
¼ teaspoon salt
1 12-ounce can (1½ cups) evaporated skim milk
3 tablespoons cooking oil
½ cup sliced fresh mushrooms
¼ cup chopped green sweet pepper
¼ cup shredded carrot
½ cup refrigerated or frozen egg product, thawed
½ teaspoon dried basil, crushed
⅛ teaspoon salt
⅛ teaspoon ground black pepper
⅔ cup shredded reduced-fat mozzarella cheese or Swiss cheese
1 tablespoon all-purpose flour

♣ In a medium saucepan combine 1½ cups *water* and the wheat berries. Bring to boiling; reduce heat. Simmer, covered, for 45 minutes to 1 hour or until tender. Drain thoroughly.

♣ Meanwhile, for pastry, in a medium mixing bowl stir together the 1¼ cups flour, ½ teaspoon basil, and ¼ teaspoon salt. In a 1-cup measure combine ¼ *cup* of the evaporated skim milk and cooking oil. Add oil mixture all at once to flour mixture. Stir lightly with a fork. Form dough into a ball. On lightly floured surface, flatten the

ball with your hands. Roll dough from center to the edge, forming a 12-inch circle. Ease pastry into a 9-inch pie plate, being careful not to stretch the pastry. Trim pastry to ½ inch beyond the edge of the pie plate. Fold the pastry under and flute the edge. *Do not prick pastry.* Line pastry shell with a double thickness of heavy-duty foil. Press down firmly but gently. Bake pastry in a 450° oven for 5 minutes; remove foil. Bake for 5 to 7 minutes more or until the pastry is nearly done and is golden. Remove from the oven. Reduce oven temperature to 325°.

♣ In a small saucepan cook mushrooms, sweet pepper, and carrot in a small amount of *boiling water* about 5 minutes or until vegetables are tender. Drain thoroughly.

♣ In a medium bowl combine the cooked vegetables, remaining evaporated milk (1¼ cups), the egg product, ½ teaspoon basil, ⅛ teaspoon salt, and the pepper. In a small bowl toss together the mozzarella or Swiss cheese and the 1 tablespoon flour. Stir into egg mixture.

♣ Sprinkle cooked wheat berries over bottom of baked pastry shell. Pour in egg mixture. Bake in 325° oven about 40 minutes or until a knife inserted near the center comes out clean. Let stand on a wire rack for 10 minutes before serving. Makes 6 main-dish servings.

Crustless Mushroom
& Carrot Quiche

To save time and reduce fat, we've eliminated the crust for this flavorful quiche. Fresh fruit or a fruit salad round it out for a light supper.

Nonstick spray coating
2 cups sliced fresh mushrooms
½ cup shredded carrot
3 eggs or ¾ cup refrigerated or frozen egg product, thawed
1 cup evaporated skim milk
1 cup shredded reduced-fat cheddar cheese (4 ounces)
1 tablespoon all-purpose flour
½ teaspoon dried dillweed
½ teaspoon dry mustard
¼ teaspoon pepper
Paprika

♣ Generously spray bottom and sides of a 9-inch pie plate with nonstick coating; set aside.

♣ Spray an unheated medium nonstick skillet with nonstick coating. Preheat over medium-high heat. Add mushrooms and carrot; stir-fry about 1 minute or just until tender. Spoon mushroom mixture into prepared pie plate, spreading evenly.

♣ In a food processor bowl or blender container combine the eggs or egg product, evaporated milk, cheddar cheese, flour, dillweed, dry mustard, and pepper. Cover and process or blend about 15 seconds or until thoroughly combined. Pour the egg mixture over mushroom mixture in the pie plate.

♣ Bake quiche in a 400° oven about 20 minutes or until a knife inserted near the center comes out clean. Sprinkle top of quiche with paprika. Let quiche stand for 5 minutes before serving. Makes 6 main-dish servings.

TOTAL FAT: 6 g
DAILY VALUE FAT: 9%
SATURATED FAT: 3 g
DAILY VALUE SATURATED FAT: 15%

NUTRITION FACTS PER SERVING:

Calories	147
Total Fat	6 g
Saturated Fat	3 g
Cholesterol	121 mg
Sodium	218 mg
Carbohydrate	9 g
Fiber	1 g
Protein	12 g

EXCHANGES:
1 Vegetable
1 Medium-Fat Meat
½ Milk

PREPARATION TIME: 12 minutes
BAKING TIME: 20 minutes
STANDING TIME: 5 minutes

Zesty Vegetable Enchiladas

For enchiladas with real gusto, be sure to include the jalapeño peppers. Substitute chopped green chilies
if you like your enchiladas milder.

½ cup dry lentils
1⅓ cups water
 2 medium carrots, thinly sliced (1 cup)
 1 medium zucchini, quartered lengthwise
     and sliced (1⅓ cups)
 1 14½-ounce can Mexican-style stewed
     tomatoes, undrained
 1 tablespoon bottled chopped jalapeño
     peppers (optional)
½ teaspoon chili powder
 8 7- to 8-inch flour tortillas
     Nonstick spray coating
½ cup shredded reduced-fat mozzarella
     cheese (2 ounces)
     Fat-free dairy sour cream (optional)
     Fresh green and/or red hot peppers
     (optional)

♣ Rinse lentils. In a medium saucepan combine lentils and water. Bring to boiling; reduce heat. Simmer, covered, for 20 minutes. Stir in carrots and zucchini. Simmer, covered, about 5 minutes more or until carrots are tender; drain. Stir in half of the *undrained* stewed tomatoes, the jalapeño peppers (if desired), and chili powder.

♣ Meanwhile, wrap the tortillas in foil. Heat in a 350° oven for 10 minutes to soften. Spray a 2-quart rectangular baking dish with nonstick coating; set aside.

♣ Divide vegetable mixture evenly among tortillas. Using *half* of the mozzarella cheese, sprinkle each of the tortillas with cheese. Roll up tortillas; place, seam sides down, in the prepared baking dish.

♣ Bake, covered, in a 350° oven for 8 minutes. Remove foil; bake for 7 to 12 minutes more or until heated through and tortillas are crisp.

♣ In a small saucepan heat the remaining stewed tomatoes. Spoon over enchiladas. Top with remaining cheese. Bake about 2 minutes more or until cheese is melted. If desired, serve with the sour cream and hot peppers. Makes 4 main-dish servings.

TOTAL FAT: 6 g
DAILY VALUE FAT: 9%
SATURATED FAT: 2 g
DAILY VALUE SATURATED FAT: 10%

NUTRITION FACTS
PER SERVING:

Calories	369
Total Fat	6 g
Saturated Fat	2 g
Cholesterol	8 mg
Sodium	665 mg
Carbohydrate	59 g
Fiber	4 g
Protein	20 g

EXCHANGES:
3 Starch
2 Vegetable
1 Lean Meat

PREPARATION TIME: 40 minutes
BAKING TIME: 17 minutes

TOTAL FAT: 11 g
DAILY VALUE FAT: 17%
SATURATED FAT: 5 g
DAILY VALUE SATURATED FAT: 25%

NUTRITION FACTS
PER SERVING:

Calories	193
Total Fat	11 g
Saturated Fat	5 g
Cholesterol	188 mg
Sodium	332 mg
Carbohydrate	9 g
Fiber	2 g
Protein	15 g

EXCHANGES:
1 Vegetables
2 Lean Meat
1 Fat

START TO FINISH: 18 minutes

Rancheros Scrambled Eggs

Cubes of lower-fat cream cheese lend a richness to otherwise plain scrambled eggs. Add fresh zucchini to canned stewed tomatoes for a simple sauce and a boost of freshness.

½ **cup chopped zucchini**
1 **teaspoon cooking oil**
1 **14½-ounce low-sodium stewed tomatoes, undrained**
1 **teaspoon chili powder**
⅛ **teaspoon ground red pepper**
8 **egg whites***
4 **eggs***
½ **cup skim milk**
½ **teaspoon onion powder**
⅛ **teaspoon salt**
⅛ **teaspoon garlic powder**
⅛ **teaspoon ground black pepper**
   Nonstick spray coating
½ **of an 8-ounce package reduced-fat cream cheese (Neufchâtel), cut into ½-inch cubes**

♣ For sauce, in a small saucepan cook zucchini in hot oil over medium heat until tender, stirring occasionally. Stir in *undrained* stewed tomatoes, chili powder, and ground red pepper. Bring to boiling; reduce heat. Boil gently, uncovered, for 8 to 10 minutes or until most of the liquid has evaporated and mixture is slightly thickened.

♣ Meanwhile, for scrambled eggs, in a large mixing bowl beat together egg whites, whole eggs, milk, onion powder, salt, garlic powder, and black pepper.

♣ Spray an unheated large nonstick skillet with nonstick coating. Preheat over medium heat. Pour egg mixture into skillet. Cook, without stirring, until mixture begins to set on the bottom and around edge. Using a spatula or a large spoon, lift and fold the partially cooked egg mixture so the uncooked portion flows underneath. Continue cooking over medium heat for 2 to 3 minutes or until egg mixture is cooked through, but is still glossy and moist. Remove from heat; immediately fold in the cream cheese cubes. Spoon scrambled eggs onto individual plates. Spoon sauce over eggs. Makes 5 main-dish servings.

*Note: You may substitute 2 cups *refrigerated or frozen egg product,* thawed, for the egg whites and whole eggs.

Fruit & Cheese Oven Omelet

Here's an ingenious way to quickly and easily serve omelets for six: Bake a huge omelet in the oven instead of cooking individual ones on top of the stove.

Nonstick spray coating
- 12 **egg whites***
- 6 **eggs***
- ¼ cup **water**
- ½ teaspoon **salt**
- ⅛ teaspoon **pepper**
- 1 cup **mixed dried fruit bits**
- 1 cup **apple juice**
- 2 tablespoons **sugar**
- ¼ teaspoon **ground nutmeg**
- 2 tablespoons **cold water**
- 1 tablespoon **cornstarch**
- 2 tablespoons **toasted chopped walnuts or pecans**
- ½ cup **shredded reduced-fat cheddar cheese (2 ounces)**

♣ Spray a 15×10×1-inch baking pan with nonstick coating; set aside.

♣ For omelet, in a large mixing bowl combine egg whites, whole eggs, the ¼ cup water, the salt, and pepper. Using a fork or a rotary beater, beat until combined but not frothy.

♣ Place the prepared baking pan on the oven rack. Carefully pour the egg white mixture into the pan. Bake in a 400° oven for 7 to 10 minutes or until the egg mixture is set but still has a glossy surface.

♣ Meanwhile, for the sauce, in a small saucepan combine the fruit bits, apple juice, sugar, and nutmeg. Bring to boiling; reduce heat. Simmer, covered, for 3 to 4 minutes or until the fruit bits are tender. In a small bowl stir together the 2 tablespoons cold water and the cornstarch; stir into mixture in saucepan. Cook and stir until thickened and bubbly. Cook and stir 1 minute more. Keep warm. Stir in nuts before serving.

♣ Cut the baked egg mixture into 6 squares measuring 5×5 inches each. Using a large spatula, remove each omelet square. Invert the omelet squares onto warm serving plates. Spoon some of the sauce onto half of each omelet; fold other half over sauce, forming a triangle or a rectangle. Sprinkle the cheddar cheese over omelets. Makes 6 main-dish servings.

***Note:** You may substitute 3 cups *refrigerated or frozen egg product,* thawed, for the egg whites and whole eggs.

TOTAL FAT: 8 g
DAILY VALUE FAT: 12%
SATURATED FAT: 3 g
DAILY VALUE SATURATED FAT: 15%

NUTRITION FACTS
PER SERVING:

Calories	256
Total Fat	8 g
Saturated Fat	3 g
Cholesterol	220 mg
Sodium	434 mg
Carbohydrate	28 g
Fiber	0 g
Protein	17 g

EXCHANGES:
2 Fruit
2 Lean Meat
½ Fat

PREPARATION TIME: 25 minutes
BAKING TIME: 8 minutes

TOTAL FAT: 8 g
DAILY VALUE FAT: 12%
SATURATED FAT: 4 g
DAILY VALUE SATURATED FAT: 20%

NUTRITION FACTS
PER SERVING:

Calories	281
Total Fat	8 g
Saturated Fat	4 g
Cholesterol	71 mg
Sodium	653 mg
Carbohydrate	36 g
Fiber	0 g
Protein	18 g

EXCHANGES:
2 Starch
1 Vegetable
1 Medium-Fat Meat

PREPARATION TIME: 25 minutes
BAKING TIME: 40 minutes
STANDING TIME: 5 minutes

Double Corn Tortilla Casserole

Delve into this Southwestern-style strata and you'll find layers of corn tortillas, mozzarella cheese, and vegetables all baked in a savory custard.

Nonstick spray coating
1½ cups frozen whole kernel corn
6 6-inch corn tortillas
1 cup shredded reduced-fat mozzarella cheese (4 ounces)
½ cup sliced green onions
1 4-ounce can diced green chili peppers, drained
¼ cup finely chopped red sweet pepper
1 cup buttermilk
2 egg whites*
1 egg*
¼ teaspoon garlic salt
⅓ cup salsa
Italian parsley (optional)

♣ Spray a 2-quart square baking dish with nonstick coating. In a medium saucepan cook corn according to package directions; drain well. Tear tortillas into bite-size pieces. Arrange *half* of the tortillas in baking dish. Top with *half* of the cheese, *half* of the corn, *half* of the green onions, *half* of the chili peppers, and *half* of the red sweet pepper. Repeat the layers using the remaining tortillas, cheese, corn, green onions, chili peppers, and sweet pepper.

♣ In a medium mixing bowl beat together the buttermilk, egg whites, whole egg, and garlic salt. Pour over tortilla mixture.

♣ Bake, uncovered, in a 325° oven about 40 minutes or until a knife inserted near the center comes out clean. Let stand for 5 minutes before serving. To serve, cut casserole into triangles. If desired, garnish with parsley. Serve with salsa. Makes 4 main-dish servings.

*Note: You may substitute ½ cup *refrigerated or frozen egg product,* thawed, for the egg whites and whole egg.

TOTAL FAT: 11 g
DAILY VALUE FAT: 17%
SATURATED FAT: 5 g
DAILY VALUE SATURATED FAT: 25%

NUTRITION FACTS
PER SERVING:

Calories	224
Total Fat	11 g
Saturated Fat	5 g
Cholesterol	132 mg
Sodium	540 mg
Carbohydrate	20 g
Fiber	0 g
Protein	13 g

EXCHANGES:
1 Starch
1 Vegetable
2 Medium-Fat Meat

PREPARATION TIME: 25 minutes
BAKING TIME: 30 minutes
STANDING TIME: 10 minutes

Greek Spinach Triangles

Using nonstick spray coating rather than butter between the sheets of phyllo dough gives a more healthful spin to this traditional Greek dish. (Pictured on page 124.)

⅔ cup chopped onion
2 tablespoons snipped fresh parsley
½ teaspoon dried oregano, crushed
¼ teaspoon ground nutmeg
¼ teaspoon pepper
2 egg whites
2 eggs
¼ cup skim milk
1 10-ounce package frozen chopped spinach, thawed and well drained
1 cup crumbled feta cheese (4 ounces)
Nonstick spray coating
5 sheets frozen phyllo dough (18×14-inch rectangle), thawed
¼ cup fat-free dairy sour cream (optional)
⅛ teaspoon lemon-pepper seasoning (optional)

♣ For filling, in a small saucepan cook the onion in a small amount of *boiling water* about 10 minutes or until very tender. Drain well. In a small bowl combine cooked onion, parsley, oregano, nutmeg, and pepper.

♣ In a medium mixing bowl combine the egg whites, whole eggs, and milk. Beat with a rotary beater or a wire whisk until smooth. Stir in onion mixture, spinach, and feta cheese.

♣ Spray the bottom of a 2-quart square baking dish with nonstick coating. Unfold phyllo sheets; cut into quarters (about 7×9 inches). (To prevent drying, keep phyllo sheets covered with plastic wrap until ready to use.) Place 1 phyllo sheet quarter in the bottom of the dish, folding as necessary to fit. Spray with nonstick coating. Repeat with 9 more quarter-sheets of phyllo and spray coating.

♣ Spread spinach mixture over the layers of phyllo in the baking dish. Layer remaining quarter-sheets of phyllo over filling, folding as necessary to fit and spraying each with nonstick coating. Using a sharp knife, score the top of the phyllo dough into 8 triangles.

♣ Bake, uncovered, in a 375° oven about 30 minutes or until golden. Let stand for 10 minutes. To serve, cut into triangles along scored lines. If desired, combine sour cream and lemon-pepper seasoning; spoon over phyllo squares. Makes 4 main-dish servings.

Broccoli-Ricotta Calzones

A twist on an Italian favorite, these chockful-of-broccoli turnovers make one terrific meal when teamed with a fresh salad.

1   10-ounce package frozen chopped
    broccoli
⅓   cup chopped onion
¼   cup shredded carrot
1   clove garlic, minced
1¼ cups fat-free ricotta cheese
¾   cup shredded reduced-fat mozzarella
    cheese (3 ounces)
2   tablespoons grated Parmesan cheese
½   teaspoon dried Italian seasoning,
    crushed
⅛   teaspoon pepper
1   10-ounce package refrigerated pizza
    dough
1   tablespoon skim milk
    Nonstick spray coating
1   tablespoon grated Parmesan cheese

♣ Cook the broccoli, onion, carrot, and garlic according to the broccoli package directions; drain well.

♣ In a large mixing bowl stir together the broccoli mixture, ricotta cheese, mozzarella cheese, the 2 tablespoons Parmesan cheese, Italian seasoning, and pepper. Unroll pizza dough. Roll or stretch dough into an 18×12-inch rectangle. Cut into six 6-inch squares. Divide broccoli mixture among squares. Brush edges of each square with milk. Lift 1 corner and stretch dough over to the opposite corner, making a triangle. With a fork, press edges of the dough well to seal.

♣ Spray a baking sheet with the nonstick coating. Arrange calzones on the baking sheet. Prick tops with a fork. Brush with milk. Sprinkle with the 1 tablespoon Parmesan cheese. Bake in a 425° oven for 12 to 15 minutes or until golden. Makes 6 main-dish servings.

TOTAL FAT: 5 g
DAILY VALUE FAT: 8%
SATURATED FAT: 2 g
DAILY VALUE SATURATED FAT: 10%

NUTRITION FACTS
PER SERVING:

Calories	205
Total Fat	5 g
Saturated Fat	2 g
Cholesterol	15 mg
Sodium	351 mg
Carbohydrate	25 g
Fiber	3 g
Protein	16 g

EXCHANGES:
1 Starch
1 Vegetable
2 Lean Meat

PREPARATION TIME: 25 minutes
BAKING TIME: 12 minutes

Tofu Pitas With Mango Salsa, recipe on page 150

Roasted Vegetable Medley With Rice,
recipe on page 142

Simply Vegetables

Versatile vegetables—any time of year—
make great main-dish meals. Dishes such
as Roasted Vegetable Medley, Sizzling
Vegetable Sandwiches, and Garden Bounty
Couscous will give you a whole new outlook
on vegetables.

TOTAL FAT: 6 g
DAILY VALUE FAT: 9%
SATURATED FAT: 1 g
DAILY VALUE SATURATED FAT: 5%

NUTRITION FACTS
PER SERVING:

Calories	411
Total Fat	6 g
Saturated Fat	1 g
Cholesterol	0 mg
Sodium	499 mg
Carbohydrate	81 g
Fiber	13 g
Protein	11 g

EXCHANGES:
5 Starch
1 Vegetable

PREPARATION TIME: 10 minutes
BAKING TIME: 40 minutes

Roasted Vegetable Medley
With Rice

Roasting the potatoes, fennel, and carrots slowly in a marjoram, vinegar, and oil dressing gives them a robust oven-browned flavor.

Nonstick spray coating
12 ounces whole tiny new potatoes, quartered
1 small fennel bulb, halved and thinly sliced
4 medium carrots, thinly bias sliced
⅓ cup vinegar
1 tablespoon water
1 tablespoon olive oil or cooking oil
2 teaspoons snipped fresh marjoram or ½ teaspoon dried marjoram, crushed
1½ teaspoons sugar
½ teaspoon celery seed
⅛ teaspoon garlic powder
1 15½-ounce can reduced-sodium garbanzo beans, rinsed and drained
1½ cups water
1½ teaspoons instant vegetable bouillon granules
1 cup jasmine rice or long grain rice
Leafy fennel tops (optional)

♣ Spray a 15×10×1-inch baking pan with nonstick coating. In pan combine the potatoes, fennel, and carrots. In a small mixing bowl stir together vinegar, 1 tablespoon water, the oil, marjoram, sugar, celery seed, and garlic powder; pour over vegetables, tossing to coat.

♣ Bake vegetables, uncovered, in 450° oven for 35 minutes, stirring once. Add garbanzo beans, tossing to combine. Bake about 5 minutes more or until vegetables are tender and beans are hot.

♣ Meanwhile, in a small saucepan bring the 2 cups water and bouillon granules to boiling. Add the uncooked rice; reduce heat. Cook, covered, for 15 to 20 minutes or until rice is tender and liquid is absorbed.

♣ To serve, fluff the rice with a fork. Serve the vegetables with the hot cooked rice. If desired, garnish with the leafy fennel tops. Makes 4 main-dish servings.

Parmesan-Style Eggplant

If you enjoy eggplant Parmesan, this healthful adaptation will become one of your favorites. Oven-browning (rather than frying) the eggplant slices and using reduced-fat mozzarella cheese make the dish low in both fat and calories.

1 small eggplant
½ cup fine dry bread crumbs
3 tablespoons grated Parmesan cheese
½ teaspoon dried Italian seasoning, crushed
1 slightly beaten egg white
1 tablespoon water
Nonstick spray coating
1 14½-ounce can Italian-style stewed tomatoes, undrained
2 teaspoons cornstarch
½ cup shredded reduced-fat mozzarella cheese (2 ounces)

♣ Peel eggplant. Cut crosswise into ½-inch-thick slices. In a shallow dish toss together the bread crumbs, Parmesan cheese, and Italian seasoning. In another shallow dish beat together the egg white and water until combined. Spray a 2-quart rectangular baking dish with nonstick coating.

♣ Dip eggplant slices into egg white mixture, then into bread crumb mixture, turning to lightly coat both sides. Place eggplant slices in a single layer in the prepared baking dish. Bake, uncovered, in a 450° oven about 15 minutes or until the eggplant is tender and golden.

♣ Meanwhile, for sauce, in a small saucepan combine *undrained* stewed tomatoes and cornstarch. Cook and stir until thickened and bubbly. Cook and stir for 2 minutes more.

♣ Spoon sauce over eggplant slices. Sprinkle slices with mozzarella cheese. Bake for 2 to 3 minutes more or until cheese is melted. Makes 4 main-dish servings.

TOTAL FAT: 4 g
DAILY VALUE FAT: 6%
SATURATED FAT: 1 g
DAILY VALUE SATURATED FAT: 5%

NUTRITION FACTS PER SERVING:

Calories	156
Total Fat	4 g
Saturated Fat	1 g
Cholesterol	9 mg
Sodium	629 mg
Carbohydrate	22 g
Fiber	2 g
Protein	10 g

EXCHANGES:
½ Starch
2 Vegetable
1 Lean Meat

PREPARATION TIME: 10 minutes
BAKING TIME: 15 minutes

TOTAL FAT: 13 g
DAILY VALUE FAT: 20%
SATURATED FAT: 2 g
DAILY VALUE SATURATED FAT: 10%

**NUTRITION FACTS
PER SERVING:**

Calories	307
Total Fat	13 g
Saturated Fat	2 g
Cholesterol	0 mg
Sodium	397 mg
Carbohydrate	41 g
Fiber	3 g
Protein	8 g

EXCHANGES:
2 Starch
2 Vegetable
2 Fat

PREPARATION TIME: 15 minutes
GRILLING TIME: 17 minutes

Sizzling Vegetable Sandwiches

Serve these colorful sandwiches no matter what the season. In warm weather, roast the veggies on the grill; in cold weather, rely on the broiler.

1 **small eggplant, cut lengthwise into
½-inch-thick slices**
1 **medium zucchini, cut lengthwise into
¼-inch-thick slices**
1 **medium yellow summer squash, cut
lengthwise into ½-inch-thick slices**
1 **medium red sweet pepper, cut into
½-inch-wide strips**
1 **small onion, cut into ½-inch-thick slices**
3 **tablespoons olive oil
Lemon-pepper seasoning**
4 **individual French rolls with sesame
seeds, halved lengthwise, or kaiser
rolls, split**
⅓ **cup plain fat-free yogurt**
¼ **teaspoon ground cumin**

♣ Brush vegetables with olive oil. Sprinkle lightly with lemon-pepper seasoning. Grill onion slices on the rack of an uncovered grill directly over medium coals for 5 minutes. Add remaining vegetables and grill for 12 to 15 minutes more or until vegetables are tender, turning once. (If some vegetables cook more quickly than others; remove and keep warm.) Grill rolls, cut sides down, about 1 minute or until lightly browned. (Or, to broil, spray the unheated rack of broiler pan with *nonstick coating.* Place the vegetables on the pan. Broil 3 to 4 inches from heat for 12 to 15 minutes or until vegetables are tender, turning once. Remove vegetables; keep warm. Toast cut sides of rolls under broiler about 30 seconds or until lightly browned.)

♣ In a small mixing bowl stir together yogurt and cumin. Layer the vegetables on bottom halves of rolls. Spoon yogurt mixture over top layer of vegetables. Cover with roll tops. Makes 4 main-dish servings.

TOTAL FAT: 4 g
DAILY VALUE FAT: 6%
SATURATED FAT: 0 g
DAILY VALUE SATURATED FAT: 0%

NUTRITION FACTS PER SERVING:

Calories	214
Total Fat	4 g
Saturated Fat	0 g
Cholesterol	0 mg
Sodium	436 mg
Carbohydrate	36 g
Fiber	3 g
Protein	11 g

EXCHANGES:
1½ Starch
1 Vegetable
1 Lean Meat

PREPARATION TIME: 30 minutes
CHILLING TIME: 1 hour
GRILLING TIME: 10 minutes

Leek & Tofu Burgers

Make these ginger-scented, heart-healthy burgers ahead of time. Chill the mixture overnight for a meal that goes together in a flash the next day.

Nonstick spray coating
1 cup sliced leeks
½ cup shredded carrot
½ teaspoon grated gingerroot
1 10½-ounce package firm light tofu (fresh bean curd)
1 slightly beaten egg white
2 tablespoons light teriyaki sauce
¾ cup fine dry bread crumbs
2 tablespoons chopped nuts, such as peanuts, pecans, or cashews
½ cup plain fat-free yogurt
¼ cup shredded zucchini
⅛ teaspoon garlic powder
6 lettuce leaves
3 large pita bread rounds, halved crosswise

♣ Spray an unheated medium skillet with nonstick coating. Preheat over medium-high heat. Add leeks, carrot, and gingerroot; cook and stir until vegetables are tender. Remove from heat; cool slightly.

♣ Drain tofu thoroughly, pressing out excess liquid. Crumble tofu into a blender container or food processor bowl. Add leek mixture, egg white, and teriyaki sauce. Cover and blend or process with several on-off turns until vegetables are finely chopped. Transfer vegetable mixture to a mixing bowl. Stir in bread crumbs and nuts. Cover and chill at least 1 hour. Shape mixture into 6 patties, about 3 inches in diameter.

♣ Spray a grill basket or broiler pan with nonstick coating. Place patties in prepared grill basket. Grill on the rack of an uncovered grill directly over medium-hot coals about 10 minutes or until heated through, turning once. (Or to broil, spray a broiler pan with nonstick coating. Place patties on the unheated rack of a broiler pan. Broil 3 to 4 inches from the heat about 10 minutes, turning patties after half of the broiling time.)

♣ Meanwhile, in a small bowl stir together the yogurt, zucchini, and garlic powder. Serve patties and lettuce leaves in pita bread halves with the yogurt mixture. Makes 6 main-dish servings.

Sweet Potato & Mushroom
Burgers

Serve the burgers plain or turn them into sandwiches by tucking them between hamburger buns or halved pita bread rounds.

1 medium sweet potato (about 6 ounces), peeled and cut into ½-inch cubes
1 medium parsnip (about 6 ounces), peeled and cut into ½-inch cubes
Nonstick spray coating
1 cup sliced fresh mushrooms
1 cup chopped onion
2 tablespoons pine nuts or chopped almonds
2 cloves garlic, minced
2 egg whites
½ cup snipped fresh parsley
¼ teaspoon salt
¼ teaspoon dried savory, crushed
1 15½-ounce can reduced-sodium garbanzo beans, rinsed and drained
1 cup fine dry bread crumbs
Leaf lettuce
6 slices tomato
⅓ cup chutney or plain fat-free yogurt

♣ In a large covered saucepan cook sweet potato and parsnip in a small amount of *boiling water* about 20 minutes or until vegetables are tender. Drain well and cool slightly.

♣ Meanwhile, spray an unheated medium skillet with nonstick coating. Preheat skillet over medium-high heat. Cook and stir mushrooms, onion, pine nuts or chopped almonds, and garlic about 5 minutes or until vegetables are tender. Cool slightly.

♣ In a food processor bowl combine mushroom mixture, egg whites, parsley, salt, and savory. Cover and process until mixture is nearly smooth. Add sweet potato-parsnip mixture and garbanzo beans. Cover and process until well combined. Transfer the mixture to a mixing bowl. Stir in bread crumbs. Shape mixture into 6 patties, about ¾-inch thick.

♣ Spray a grill basket with nonstick coating. Place patties in prepared grill basket. Grill on the rack of an uncovered grill directly over medium-hot coals about 10 minutes or until cooked through, turning basket once. (Or, if desired, spray an unheated large skillet with nonstick coating. Preheat over medium heat on range top; add patties. Cook about 10 minutes or until lightly browned and cooked through, turning once.) Serve on lettuce leaf with a tomato slice; top with some of the chutney or yogurt. Makes 6 main-dish servings.

TOTAL FAT: 4 g
DAILY VALUE FAT: 6%
SATURATED FAT: 1 g
DAILY VALUE SATURATED FAT: 5%

NUTRITION FACTS PER SERVING:

Calories	247
Total Fat	4 g
Saturated Fat	1 g
Cholesterol	0 mg
Sodium	323 mg
Carbohydrate	46 g
Fiber	7 g
Protein	9 g

EXCHANGES:
2½ Starch
1 Vegetable

PREPARATION TIME: 40 minutes
GRILLING TIME: 10 minutes

Fettuccine With Grilled Vegetables

If you are using wooden skewers, soak them in water overnight to prevent them from burning on the hot grill. For an eye-catching presentation, arrange the grilled vegetables over a combination of plain and spinach fettuccine.

1 small eggplant, peeled and cut into 1-inch pieces

2 large fresh portobello mushrooms, stems removed, cut into 1½-inch pieces

1 large green sweet pepper, cut into 1-inch pieces

½ cup dry white wine

¼ cup water

2 teaspoons instant vegetable bouillon granules

1 tablespoon cornstarch

1 tablespoon snipped fresh basil or 1 teaspoon dried basil, crushed

2 teaspoons snipped fresh savory or ½ teaspoon dried savory, crushed

2 teaspoons snipped fresh thyme or ½ teaspoon dried thyme, crushed

8 ounces packaged dried spinach fettuccine or plain fettuccine

1 small tomato, chopped (½ cup)

½ cup shredded reduced-fat mozzarella cheese (2 ounces)

2 tablespoons finely shredded Parmesan cheese

¼ teaspoon freshly ground black pepper

♣ Thread the eggplant cubes, mushroom pieces, and sweet pepper pieces alternately onto eight 12-inch-long skewers; set aside.

♣ For sauce, in a saucepan combine wine, water, bouillon granules, cornstarch, basil, savory, and thyme. Bring to boiling; reduce heat. Cook and stir until thickened and bubbly; cook and stir for 1 minute more. Keep warm.

♣ Brush kabobs with 1 to 2 tablespoons sauce. Grill kabobs on the rack of an uncovered grill directly over medium coals for 8 to 10 minutes or until vegetables are just tender, turning once. (Or, to broil kabobs, spray an unheated broiler pan with nonstick coating. Place the kabobs on broiler pan. Broil 3 to 4 inches from the heat for 8 to 10 minutes or until vegetables are crisp-tender, turning once.) Meanwhile, cook pasta according to package directions, *except* omit any oil or salt. Drain and keep warm.

♣ To serve, toss pasta with remaining wine sauce and arrange on 4 dinner plates. Slide the vegetables from skewers onto each serving of pasta. Sprinkle each serving with chopped tomato, mozzarella cheese, Parmesan cheese, and black pepper. Makes 4 main-dish servings.

TOTAL FAT: 5 g
DAILY VALUE FAT: 7%
SATURATED FAT: 2 g
DAILY VALUE SATURATED FAT: 10%

NUTRITION FACTS
PER SERVING:

Calories	354
Total Fat	5 g
Saturated Fat	2 g
Cholesterol	10 mg
Sodium	583 mg
Carbohydrate	58 g
Fiber	3 g
Protein	16 g

EXCHANGES:
3 Starch
2 Vegetable
1 Lean Meat

START TO FINISH: 30 minutes

TOTAL FAT: 2 g
DAILY VALUE FAT: 3%
SATURATED FAT: 0 g
DAILY VALUE SATURATED FAT: 0%

NUTRITION FACTS
PER SERVING:

Calories	175
Total Fat	2 g
Saturated Fat	0 g
Cholesterol	0 mg
Sodium	214 mg
Carbohydrate	33 g
Fiber	3 g
Protein	7 g

EXCHANGES:

1 Starch
1 Fruit
1 Lean Meat

PREPARATION TIME: 35 minutes
GRILLING TIME: 10 minutes

Tofu Pitas With Mango Salsa

Although the ingredients for Jamaican jerk seasoning differ from brand to brand, this Caribbean flavoring blend typically includes chili peppers, thyme, garlic, and onion. Look for it in the seasoning aisle of your supermarket.

2 **tablespoons lime juice or lemon juice**
1 **teaspoon cooking oil**
½ **teaspoon Jamaican jerk seasoning**
1 **10½-ounce package firm light tofu (fresh bean curd)**
  Nonstick spray coating
⅓ **cup couscous**
3 **large pita bread rounds, halved crosswise**
  Fresh spinach leaves or torn lettuce leaves
1 **recipe Mango Salsa**
  Lime slices (optional)

♣ In a shallow dish or pie plate combine the lime or lemon juice, cooking oil, and Jamaican jerk seasoning. Slice tofu into ½-inch-thick slices. Lay slices in marinade and brush marinade over tofu slices. Let stand at room temperature for 30 minutes, turning slices once and brushing marinade over all; or, marinate in refrigerator for up to 6 hours.

♣ Spray a grill basket with nonstick coating. Place tofu slices in prepared grill basket. Discard marinade. Grill tofu slices in basket on the rack of an uncovered grill directly over medium-hot coals about 10 minutes or until heated through. Cut the slices of tofu into cubes. (Or, if desired,

spray an unheated broiler pan with nonstick coating. Lay tofu slices on the broiler pan. Broil tofu 5 to 6 inches from the heat about 8 minutes or until heated through, turning once.)

♣ Meanwhile, cook couscous according to package directions, *except* omit the added butter and salt. Fluff couscous with fork. To serve, add tofu cubes and couscous to Mango Salsa, tossing gently to combine. Line pita halves with spinach or lettuce leaves. Spoon salsa mixture into pita halves. If desired, garnish with lime slices. Makes 6 main-dish servings

Mango Salsa: In a large bowl combine 1 cup chopped, peeled, and seeded *mango;* 1 small *tomato,* seeded and chopped; ½ of a medium *cucumber,* seeded and chopped; 1 thinly sliced *green onion;* 2 tablespoons snipped fresh *cilantro;* 1 fresh *jalapeño pepper,** seeded and chopped; and 1 tablespoon *lime* or *lemon juice.* Cover and chill until serving time. Makes about 2 cups.

***Note:** Protect your hands when working with hot peppers by wearing plastic or rubber gloves or working with plastic bags on your hands. If your bare hands touch the peppers, wash your hands and under your nails thoroughly with soap and water. Avoid rubbing your mouth, nose, eyes, or ears when working with hot peppers.

Barley With Chayote

Pale green and pear-shaped, chayote (chaw-YOTE-ee) is actually a fruit that tastes like a mild squash. Most readily available during the winter months, it might be labeled with its French name, mirliton, at your supermarket.

1 chayote (about 12-ounces), cut into ½-inch cubes
1 cup water
⅓ cup quick-cooking barley
¼ cup thinly sliced green onions
¼ cup mixed dried fruit bits
1 teaspoon instant vegetable bouillon granules
½ teaspoon curry powder
¼ cup slivered almonds, toasted, or coarsely chopped peanuts

♣ In a medium saucepan combine chayote, water, barley, green onions, mixed fruit bits, bouillon granules, and curry powder. Bring to boiling; reduce heat. Simmer, covered, for 10 to 12 minutes or until barley is tender and broth is absorbed. Sprinkle with almonds or peanuts. Makes 3 main-dish servings.

The Many Facets of Curry

Curry is actually not a single spice. Typically used in Indian cooking, curry is a blend of as many as 20 spices, herbs, and seeds, which may include cumin, cardamom, coriander, red pepper, fenugreek, ginger, and turmeric. Cinnamon, cloves, allspice, and fennel seed also may be used. Turmeric gives curry dishes their distinguishing yellow color. Try to use ground curry soon after you buy it, as it loses its flavor in about six months or sooner.

If a recipe calling for curry is not going to be cooked, you may want to cook the curry powder in a little oil or butter before using it, to avoid a harsh, raw flavor.

TOTAL FAT: 5 g
DAILY VALUE FAT: 7%
SATURATED FAT: 0 g
DAILY VALUE SATURATED FAT: 0%

NUTRITION FACTS PER SERVING:

Calories	178
Total Fat	5 g
Saturated Fat	0 g
Cholesterol	0 mg
Sodium	301 mg
Carbohydrate	30 g
Fiber	4 g
Protein	6 g

EXCHANGES:
1½ Starch
1 Vegetable
½ Fat

START TO FINISH: 25 minutes

TOTAL FAT: 5 g
DAILY VALUE FAT: 7%
SATURATED FAT: 2 g
DAILY VALUE SATURATED FAT: 10%

NUTRITION FACTS
PER SERVING:

Calories	351
Total Fat	5 g
Saturated Fat	2 g
Cholesterol	11 mg
Sodium	468 mg
Carbohydrate	59 g
Fiber	14 g
Protein	18 g

EXCHANGES:
3 Starch
2 Vegetable
1 Lean Meat

START TO FINISH: 30 minutes

Garden Bounty Couscous

Although couscous looks like a grain, it is actually tiny pasta. In Morocco, where it originated, it is prepared with a variety of vegetables and meats and is served in some form at almost every meal.

1 cup water
2 medium carrots, bias-sliced (1 cup)
1 medium onion, chopped (½ cup)
1 teaspoon vegetable bouillon granules
1½ cups fresh pea pods, halved crosswise
1 15½-ounce can reduced-sodium garbanzo beans, rinsed and drained
1 cup couscous
½ cup skim milk
1 tablespoon snipped fresh savory or
  1 teaspoon dried savory, crushed
¼ teaspoon garlic powder
⅛ teaspoon pepper
½ cup shredded reduced-fat Monterey Jack cheese (2 ounces)

♣ In a medium saucepan combine the water, carrots, onion, and vegetable bouillon granules. Bring to boiling; reduce heat. Simmer, covered, for 6 minutes. Stir in the pea pods. Continue cooking, covered, about 3 minutes more or until vegetables are just crisp-tender.

♣ Stir in the garbanzo beans, couscous, milk, savory, garlic powder, and pepper. Heat just to boiling. Remove from heat; cover and let stand for 5 minutes. Divide mixture among 4 bowls or plates. Sprinkle with Monterey Jack cheese. Makes 4 main-dish servings.

Cleaner Beans?

Many of the recipes in this book call for the canned beans to be rinsed. No, it's not to make them squeaky clean. Although beans are a great source of fiber and protein, canned beans tend to be high in sodium. Rinsing helps wash off the canning liquid, which is the source of the sodium. To rinse canned beans, place them in a colander and rinse them thoroughly with cold water before using.

You also can purchase reduced-sodium canned beans. Not all varieties of canned beans are available in reduced-sodium versions, but, generally, any bean variety can be substituted for another in recipes.

We've taken the hassle out of planning a tasty meal for you and your family. Here's more than a week's worth of menus to get you started on eating low-fat meals—the vegetarian way.

Asparagus Potato Scramble, page 14
Mixed fresh fruit
Lentil-Rice Breakfast Patties, page 17

Barley Bean Salad, page 53
Bread sticks
Fruit sorbet

The New Chef's Salad, page 61
Whole wheat crackers
Angel food cake topped with fruit

Minestrone, page 66
Italian bread
Fresh mixed greens salad

Mexican-Style Pasta, page 96
Fresh mixed greens salad
Chocolate pudding

Sizzling Vegetable Sandwiches, page 144
Baked sweet potato chips
Purchased cookies

Triple Mushroom and Rice Fajitas, page 111
Low-fat vegetarian refried beans
Purchased brownies

Double Corn Tortilla Casserole, page 136
Mixed bean salad
Low-fat pound cake topped
with mixed berries

Metric Cooking Hints

By making a few conversions, cooks in Australia, Canada, and the United Kingdom can use the recipes in *Better Homes and Gardens® Low-fat & Luscious Vegetarian* with confidence. The charts on this page provide a guide for converting measurements from the U.S. customary system, which is used throughout this book, to the imperial and metric systems. There also is a conversion table for oven temperatures to accommodate the differences in oven calibrations.

Volume and Weight: Americans traditionally use cup measures for liquid and solid ingredients. The chart (top right) shows the approximate imperial and metric equivalents. If you are accustomed to weighing solid ingredients, here are some helpful approximate equivalents:
- 1 cup butter, castor sugar, or rice = 8 ounces = about 250 grams
- 1 cup flour = 4 ounces = about 125 grams
- 1 cup icing sugar = 5 ounces = about 150 grams

Spoon measures are used for smaller amounts of ingredients. Although the size of the tablespoon varies slightly among countries, for practical purposes and for recipes in this book, a straight substitution is all that's necessary.

Measurements made using cups or spoons should always be level, unless stated otherwise.

Product Differences: Most of the ingredients called for in the recipes in this book are available in English-speaking countries. However, some are known by different names. Here are some common American ingredients and the possible counterparts:
- Sugar is granulated or castor sugar.
- Powdered sugar is icing sugar.
- All-purpose flour is plain household flour or white flour. When self-rising flour is used in place of all-purpose flour in a recipe that calls for leavening, omit the leavening agent (baking soda or baking powder) and salt.
- Light corn syrup is golden syrup.
- Cornstarch is cornflour.
- Baking soda is bicarbonate of soda.
- Vanilla is vanilla essence.

Useful Equivalents

⅛ teaspoon = 0.5 ml	⅔ cup = 5 fluid ounces = 150 ml
¼ teaspoon = 1 ml	¾ cup = 6 fluid ounces = 175 ml
½ teaspoon = 2 ml	1 cup = 8 fluid ounces = 250 ml
1 teaspoon = 5 ml	2 cups = 1 pint
¼ cup = 2 fluid ounces = 50 ml	2 pints = 1 litre
⅓ cup = 3 fluid ounces = 75 ml	½ inch = 1 cm
½ cup = 4 fluid ounces = 125 ml	1 inch = 2 cm

Baking Pan Sizes

American	Metric
8×1½-inch round baking pan	20×4-cm sandwich or cake tin
9×1½-inch round baking pan	23×3.5-cm sandwich or cake tin
11×7×1½-inch baking pan	28×18×4-cm baking pan
13×9×2-inch baking pan	32.5×23×5-cm baking pan
2-quart rectangular baking dish	30×19×5-cm baking pan
15×10×2-inch baking pan	38×25.5×2.5-cm baking pan (Swiss roll tin)
9-inch pie plate	22×4- or 23×4-cm pie plate
7- or 8-inch springform pan	18- or 20-cm springform or loose-bottom cake tin
9×5×3-inch loaf pan narrow loaf pan or paté tin	23×13×6-cm or 2-pound
1½-quart casserole	1.5-litre casserole
2-quart casserole	2-litre casserole

Oven Temperature Equivalents

Fahrenheit Setting	Celsius Setting*	Gas
300°F	150°C	Gas Mark 2
325°F	160°C	Gas Mark 3
350°F	180°C	Gas Mark 4
375°F	190°C	Gas Mark 5
400°F	200°C	Gas Mark 6
425°F	220°C	Gas Mark 7
450°F	230°C	Gas Mark 8
Broil		Grill

Electric and gas ovens may be calibrated using Celsius. However, increase the Celsius setting 10 to 20 degrees when cooking above 160°C with an electric oven. For convection or forced-air ovens (gas or electric), lower the temperature setting 10°C when cooking at all heat levels.